BEVEL DOWN
The absurd tragic mcmoir of an Okie meth head.
By
Todd Langley

Much of this story is true. Much is not.
The names have been changed to protect the guilty
as well as the innocent.

LOGAN COUNTY, OKLAHOMA APRIL 1995

CHAPTER 1

When I swaggered into the Texaco the first thing I took note of was the clerk. To my satisfaction he was busily ringing up purchases of cigarettes, beer, snacks, and petrol. I had waited for a decent rush of after five o'clock working stiffs to keep him occupied while I did my work in the bathroom. I remember thinking that the patrons looked like any typical spattering of the walking dead that made up society at large. As far as I was concerned most people were a parade of fools that blindly labored their lives away for nothing.

Considering the fact that I was a thieving junkie who had been awake for five days straight, there was a heavy dose of irony in both of these thoughts.

I was well aware of the irony and relished it. There was no shame in my game. I thrived on the delusion that I was no mere criminal, but a bona fide outlaw who played by his own rules in a world gone mad.

I adjusted my shades and headed toward the bathroom, uncontrollably eyeing the shelves yet resisting the spontaneous urge to pocket some merchandise. I had to stay focused. This was a mission that entailed more than mere shoplifting.

Delighted to find the bathroom unoccupied, I quickly entered. The door was soon closed behind me then locked. I tried to open it to make sure it was locked. Indeed it was. I then unlocked the door and opened it briefly before closing it, locking it once more, and again trying to open it to make sure it was locked. Finally satisfied, I turned and looked in the mirror. I removed my shades. My hollow eyes and thin face made me look like I was almost thirty years old.

I was nineteen.

I grinned, and my hideous reflection grinned toothily back. I could have stood there for an hour playing mirror mirror on the wall, contemplating the elasticity of consciousness and its effects on human facial features, but I again reminded myself to stay focused.

I took off the flannel shirt I wore despite the balmy seventy five degree day. Its purpose was not warmth, but to hide the needle marks on my forearms. I hung the shirt on a hook, and my slightly shaky hands reached into the deep recesses of my baggy pants to pull out a ratchet and an assortment of sockets. Next, I carefully lined the sockets in a row on the back of the toilet and looked closely at what was the back wall of the gas station. A line of bolts dotted a vertical seam where two sheets of the corrugated aluminum came together. I grabbed what looked to be the correct sized socket and tried to fit it over one of the nuts.

Bingo.

I inserted the ratchet into the back of the socket and went to work relieving the bolts of their respective nuts. It was the kind of work every meth head was good at. Repetitive tasks were the forte of any speed freak. We could spend hours wiling away the time sharpening knives, loading clips, or picking at scabs.

I was almost done with my task when a sharp knock rapped on the bathroom door. I almost jumped out of my skin.

"Occupied," I hollered before turning to open up the faucet in the small sink full blast. The sound of rushing water drowned out the more suspicious tones of the ratchet, and I quickly finished removing the nuts. My friend Barry was waiting outside in my car. I knew I had already been in here long enough for him to be getting anxious. I could see him in my mind, sitting in the passenger seat chain smoking hand rolled cigarettes, trying not to convince himself my mischief had been discovered.

The last nut popped off. I dropped it into a pocket with the rest and rounded up my tools. I threw on my flannel and placed the shades back over my caved peepers before turning the water off. I gave the haunted countenance in the mirror a quick smirk and again jumped when the knock returned, louder this time. I immediately yanked the door open and flew past an impatient blue collar slug, ignoring the baleful glare he shot at the long haired dreg that oozed by him. I was used to such looks from the common folk, and they no longer penetrated the thick armor I had grown around my self image. I believed my heart was a stone that no chisel could dent or even scratch.

Little did I know at the time it was not chisels that most effectively wore away stone, but that devastating combination of fire and water.

I stepped outside after purchasing a pack of Marlboro Reds with the handful of quarters I had left from my robbery the night before, which was a twenty four hour laundromat. I used a tire iron to smash open a few change boxes and acquired enough silver for ten bucks in gas, a half gram of crank, and the cigarettes I'd just bought.

Presently, I could see my partner Barry's squat but broad frame sitting in the rundown Chevy I had inherited from my grandma. My schizophrenic, drug addicted mother had hoped I would use it to get a job since I had dropped out of school. The freedom of owning a vehicle instead prompted me to leave home altogether. I hadn't seen or talked to my mom in over a year.

I smacked the pack against my palm as I walked to the car, then casually tossed the cellophane to the ground before opening the door and plopping down next to Barry. The tense look on his stubborn face said I had been gone for eons, and he had wondered if he should just bail on this whole idiotic scheme.

"About goddamn time," he said, confirming my suspicion. I thumped a tailor made from the pack and offered it to him. He chucked the rollie he'd been puffing out the window and snagged the Class A.

"I would 'a been quicker, but I had to take a shit," I informed him. He laughed emptily at my wit, still unnerved by the long wait in the car.

"You sure you got all those nuts off? We can't be banging on that fucking wall at 3 a.m."

My jaw reflexively clenched. I didn't like being doubted.

"The bolts were in a straight line. No mazes or geometric intricacies to speak of. So yeah, I'm pretty sure I got 'em all. You can go on in and inspect my work if you got your panties in a bunch. Just don't mind the smell."

A dark sparkle briefly glinted in my friend's eyes before passing as quickly as it came. It was dangerous to patronize Barry, but my easy manner and dry wit made me one of the few people who could get away with it. It also helped that he didn't currently have his own car and often needed me to give him rides on his errands.

"That's what I like about you, Todd. Even when you've been going for a few days, you still keep it together."

Barry took a deep drag off his smoke. I started the car and pulled out of the parking lot to join the flow of traffic. My hand began tapping the steering wheel in a constant motion, a sure sign I was thinking about my next fix.

"We should do another blast before tonight if we're gonna be on our toes. We got much left?" I asked.

Barry pulled a small plastic bag from his pocket and examined its meager contents. The dark sparkle returned to his eyes.

"We got a little. Hollister's bags have been getting lighter and lighter. I'm gonna have to have a talk with him real soon."

I doubted there would be much actual talking in that exchange. Hollister was the only local guy who knew how to cook, but Barry was the crazy bastard no one dared cross. They had once been tight friends, and not so long ago Barry was Holly's right hand man, but their relationship had grown increasingly worse over the last couple months. It was a common occurrence amongst peers in our world.

I often wondered how long it would take for me and Barry's friendship to sour as well. The dumber part of me, the part that wanted to take a flamethrower to the candle of life, reasoned that as long as there was a steady supply of the ambrosia our mutual veins desired then things would be swell. The wiser part knew that when the time of plenty passed there would be fighting over the scraps. Even though I was making some money hustling quarter papers, grams, and teeners with Barry, we often did more than we sold, and so I was doing up to three or four minor larcenies a week to keep the cash coming in. To my credit, I was very particular about the kinds of places I would rob from. Houses were off limits. Being an unauthorized presence in someone's home is a very uncomfortable feeling for me, as I suspect it is for most sensible folk. Businesses, on the other hand, were public by nature, and I had no problem giving them a financial trim.

All in all it was exciting and challenging work, but it was quite hazardous and required long hours.

"God damn that thing is loud."

Barry looked around nervously while my ratchet once again was put to use, this time outside the station. It was almost four in the morning, and all was dead quiet except for the fast rat-a-tat-tat of my spinning tool.

"It's not that loud. There's no houses back here," I patiently assured him. Indeed, the lot behind the station was empty, which left us feeling somewhat exposed, but the absence of any light kept us hidden in the shadow of the building. The station was basically one big aluminum box with a front window and glass door. I was pretty sure the outside seam I was working on would open up close to where I had undone the bolts from the inside. My biggest concern was passing through the one foot of space in between. If we ran into pipes or electrical wires we might not be able to go through. Of course, I didn't tell Barry that. He was wound up enough as it was.

"You sure they don't have any motion detectors or something in there?" he asked, voicing his own concerns.

"Nope," I answered frankly. "But I know they probably wouldn't bother installing the cheap sensors I saw on the window and the door if they had motion detectors."

Barry was only mildly satisfied with this logic. He didn't like being a thief in the night anyway, especially in his own neighborhood, which was a sad two mile square of trailer houses and Section 8 homes near the town of Edmond that everyone charmingly called Felony Flats. Barry had grown up there, and his standing in the community could be summed up by one word – notorious. He was often blamed for the things he didn't do, much the less the ones he did. Police in two counties knew him on a first name basis.

I, on the other hand, was a homeless transplant who had only been hanging out in the Flats for the past six months. I had discovered this odd neighborhood after reconnecting with my best friend Desmond. He had moved a couple towns away over a year before, about the time my own life had spiraled into chaos. When I ran into his cousin at a pool hall I got Desmond's new number. After calling and catching up on things, he got his mom to talk his new stepdad Gerald into letting me stay with them if I got a job. No job manifested, and when Gerald caught me taking money out of his wallet he tried to throttle me. Fortunately, I am slippery as an eel and fast as a cheetah, so I escaped bodily harm, but needless to say that bridge was burned. Desmond was still a friend, he had no love for his stepdad, but I was effectively back on the streets. Once I was adrift in the Flats it took little time to acquaint myself with Barry and his circle of outcasts. Birds of a feather.

I finished the last nut, let it fall to the ground, and dropped the ratchet into a pocket. I got my fingers under the seam and gripped the edge with both hands.

"You ready?" I asked.

Barry nodded but offered no words.

"Grab this edge with me. It's gonna be loud, but if we yank it back fast it won't be loud for long."

I examined Barry's sweaty intense face. He was a valuable friend to have, but this type of work wasn't in him. If he wanted to take something, Barry would rather take it by brute force in broad daylight. That was more his style, not this slinking about.

As for me, robbing a lone outpost of a big company like Texaco fit nicely with the image of myself as an outlaw. Barry was an idealist too, but of a different sort. I was more the renegade philosopher, whereas Barry embodied a maniacal conqueror. Of course, both of those archetypes were doused with a turbulent methamphetamine sauce and placed on a chess table where the pieces were not elegant lords and ladies but poor white trash.

When we pulled on the siding it peeled back with a dull screech that made us both grimace.

"Now just hold it a sec," I said. Barry did as he was told while his head swiveled in stark paranoia.

"You just better be right about this score," he said through clenched teeth.

I ignored his whining and placed my body in the now exposed gap. I peered into the space between the walls and was pleased to see no major obstructions. I put my foot against the outside wall so Barry could let go, and then dug a small flashlight from my back pocket. I shined it at the inner wall and saw the inside seam. I pushed on it with my free hand.

The wall parted. I laughed aloud and shone my light through. Barry came up behind me and peaked in to see the inside of the bathroom. I turned to him and grinned.

"At any rate, I'll bet ya there ain't no motion detectors in the shitter."

3

"Nine hundred and thirty two dollars and twenty three cents."

I laid the stack on the car seat between me and Barry. Once we were inside everything went smooth. No motion detectors and no safe to deal with. I found the money wrapped with a rubber band behind the tray in the register. It wasn't the first time I'd found money hidden in such a way. I could only guess as to why business owners thought this was clever. I reckoned they thought your average burglar was too stupid to look in such an obvious place. Not this kid.

In addition to the cash, we filled two garbage bags with twenty cartons of cigarettes, thirteen lighters, two pairs of sunglasses, six quarts of motor oil, and a box of Snickers. It was a sweet score to say the least.

"What does that make it apiece?" asked Barry. It only took me a second to do the math in my head. I was always good with numbers.

"Four hundred sixty six dollars and eleven and a half cents," I told him.

"I see. Well, I'm feeling generous so you can have the half cent, and we'll just call it even," Barry replied with a smile.

"What a guy," I said and began splitting up the take. Barry lit a fresh stogie and kicked back. We were parked in the narrow graveled alley behind his parent's trailer house. He was twenty three and lived at home with them and his eighteen year old brother Cass.

"How long have we been going?" he asked.

"About six days," I replied, trying not to lose count on the divvy.

"It's been a good run."

"Amen to that," I said, and laid the last one on Barry's stack. I handed it to him, and he took it with pleasure.

"You might want to count it again. I'm pretty sure it's right, but I ain't seeing all that straight," I told him quite honestly. He didn't look too concerned about it though. He stuffed the cash into his pocket without even looking at it.

"I'll count it when I wake up in two days. If it feels light I'll kick your ass later," he said.

"Fair enough," I returned, knowing full well he wouldn't remember the tally by the time he woke up. Hell, I probably wouldn't remember it either.

"You gonna crash in your car out by the lake or get a hotel?" Barry asked.

"Neither," I said. "The sun's coming up so I think I'll go over to Desmond's and pass out on his floor."

"I thought ole Gerald wanted to wring your scrawny neck?"

"He works from dawn till dusk on an oil rig. I'll park around the block, and it'll all be good. Dez lets me crash in the closet. At least I'll get a few hours sleep in the dark."

In retrospect this would turn out to be a bad call on my part, but I was out of dope, and my vision was starting to blur. Previous experience told me I was fading fast, and I didn't think I could make it all the way out to the interstate to get a hotel without crashing into the ditch. Such are the woes of real life vampires.

"Alright then, I'm out," Barry drawled. We shook hands.

"I'll pop the trunk so you can grab your share of the smokes," I said.

"Good deal," he replied.

Barry shuffled lazily out and walked around to the back of the car. I hit the button that was supposed to open the trunk lid, half expecting it to fail. It had been on the fritz lately, but this time it worked just fine. The lid popped up, and Barry took his haul. He closed the lid, and I watched him shamble around the side of the trailer with the trash bag of cigarettes hung over his shoulder like a macabre Santa.

Then I started the car and drove to Desmond's for what would be a less than stellar day's sleep.

CHAPTER 2

The muffled sound of breaking dishes clattered in the back of my sleep fogged mind. The sound was soon followed by the blunt crash of a body being shoved hard into a wall. As I climbed toward consciousness I heard yelling in the next room; an angry man's voice and one belonging to a scared woman.

The distinct, hard slap of flesh on flesh penetrated my ears. I sat up in the darkness, listening, suddenly fully awake. The angry man bellowed, his voice full of rage.

"What the hell have you been doin' all God damn day?"

I had time to realize the voice belonged to Gerald before I heard another blunt crash, and then Sylvia blurting out, "I was helping Cole with his homework! I lost track of the time. Please don't do this while he's visitin'. Please."

Again came the blunt crash as he shoved her back into the wall. I could hear Gerald mumble something unintelligible yet menacing. To this day the memory of that sound makes my skin crawl. I later learned that what had set Gerald off was the fact that he had come home for lunch, and Sylvia didn't have it ready yet.

I heard Sylvia half demand, half beg, "Gerald, stop this. Stop this right now."

I reached up and felt for the long string that hung from the light on the ceiling. I was holed up in Desmond's closet. I didn't know it at the time, but I had been out for almost two days. When I tugged the cord the closet illuminated in a soft 40 watt glow. My eyes throbbed as they adjusted to the light. I pushed the door open and peaked out to see if Desmond was around. It looked like he was asleep in his bed.

"You awake, Desmond?"

Desmond answered in his usual dry tone.

"Yeah. I'm awake."

"What should we do?"

He didn't answer. He rolled over and reached for a pack of smokes that sat atop a milk crate next to a pair of glasses and an overfilled ashtray. He fingered a smoke out of the pack. Mingled with the crinkle of the soft pack came the sound of another hard slap; followed by a low moan from Sylvia.

Desmond's expression remained relatively blank at the sound of his mother being struck, but I now know his dark moody eyes and casual movements were signs of a huge swell before it crested and crashed into the shore. He held his long black hair aside and lit his smoke.

I was not sharing my friend's need to appear calm.

"We need to go out there and stop this shit right now."

Desmond exhaled and replied, "I'm not going anywhere."

I'd like to say that I couldn't believe my ears, but the hard fact is that I'm pretty sure Desmond had gotten used to this kind of thing over the years. It was the type of conditioning that could leave you feeling helpless and apathetic, even if you were as smart and savvy as Desmond. There is no formal education on how to deal with shit like that.

Before I could find the words to reply, Gerald's voice raged from beyond.

"You are a worthless fucking woman!"

Sylvia cried out as she was pummeled. Our ears were bombarded by meaty thuds as Gerald lost restraint. I couldn't handle it. I rose to my feet, eyes wide, and my heart pounding in my chest.

"This is fucked up."

Desmond nodded.

"Yes, it is."

"What should we do?"

"I don't know." He took a deep drag off his smoke.

My jaw clenched. I didn't like that answer.

"I think we should go out there. Right now."

Desmond exhaled. "Gerald is bigger than both of us put together."

He was right about that. Gerald was a big strong motherfucker. He'd probably cripple me, but I couldn't just sit there.

"God damn it. I wish I'd gotten a hotel."

I went for the door and heard Desmond speak more to himself than to me.

"If I had a choice I wouldn't be here either."

A shotgun blast boomed through the trailer house and rattled the aluminum siding.

I was stopped dead in my tracks. I took a step back and looked at Desmond. His hand went limp, and his cigarette fell to the floor. Every fiber of dust and pale light in the room seemed to hang suspended.

Sylvia screamed, breaking the spell.

Desmond realized his error and stomped out the cigarette. My hand tightened on the door knob again.

"Holy shit. Your mom shot him. She fucking shot him." I whispered.

Desmond got his ass in gear. He grabbed his glasses, leaped off the bed, and shoved me aside. He yanked the door open and flew out with me close behind. We hustled down the short hallway and past the kitchen to the living room.

The scene we arrived to see was even more chaotic than imagined. Broken things were everywhere. Mostly dishes, knick knacks, pictures of happier times. Gerald lay on his side staring at the floor and gasped. He bled almost black blood from a wound below his ribcage and cried as he spoke to a God he had little right to beseech.

"Dear Jesus. Oh holy Jesus. Oh Jesus…"

Sylvia sat silent, her eyes glazed and gazing at the broken man on the floor in front of her. Her raven hair fell in a wreck around her battered and bloodied face. Her delicate but stern Cheyenne features twitched with shock.

Desmond approached slowly, trying to process what he beheld. He put his hand on her shoulder and bent down until he could see into her eyes. After a moment she registered his presence. She spoke.

"It was Cole. Cole shot him."

Her eyes filled with tears, and she buried her head in her son's arms. Desmond absorbed the fact that his eleven year old brother was the shooter. His dark eyes reflected unknown depths of inner turmoil.

I later thought it was strange that I was the one who picked up the phone from the kitchen wall and dialed 911, but I did it nonetheless. No other possibility even crossed my mind. In the handful of seconds I stood waiting on the line I heard Desmond mutter under his breath.

"Cole. Holy shit."

I got an operator and stated point blank, "Somebody here's been shot." I then gave a curt answer when the dispatcher asked if there was still a present danger "No, there's no danger. A little kid shot his stepdad 'cause he was hitting his mamma. Just send the ambulance. 89405 North Waterloo Road."

I hung up the phone and walked into the living room. Desmond sat on the couch and held his mom. I stared at the fallen Gerald. He still pleaded with divinity.

"Forgive me. Please God forgive me."

I felt a sympathy I didn't quite understand. I found myself going to the kitchen and grabbing a hand towel off its hook. I wet it at the sink and returned to Gerald, then knelt down and placed the cool rag over the open wound in his side. My eyes noticed that he also bled from the hand and forearm in what I knew forensics folks called defensive wounds.

Gerald looked up, eyes swimming near the void.

"What are you doing?"

I shook my head in wonder and answered bluntly.

"Trying to help your sorry ass, but I'll be damned if I know why."

I felt a presence beside me and turned to see Desmond, who looked down unemotionally at his dying stepfather. Gerald somehow felt the gaze. He raised his eyes to Desmond, looking at him directly. Gerald told him the score.

"I'm going to die."

Desmond nodded somberly.

"Good."

Gerald's face flushed red at Desmond's callous answer, but he said nothing, only returned his gaze to the unknown. Silent tears streamed down his face.

Desmond looked down at him as if studying a particularly nasty pile of shit. He'd suffered Gerald's abuse along with his mother for the past year and half they'd been together. This moment was a bittersweet one for him to say the least. It was the first time I ever saw his eyes wet with emotion. Regardless, I felt the need to ask an important question.

"Where's Cole?"

Desmond looked at me and had to think only for a second before replying.

"I know where he is."

I was about to say that we should probably go find him when we heard the sound of a siren rising in the distance. I cringed at the sound, knowing it was too soon for the ambulance and was therefore some cop who had been cruising the Flats.

"I really should have just gotten a hotel."

Desmond was quite familiar with my frequent flouting of the law, as well as my addictions. He had witnessed much of the behavior as it developed. Minus the year I'd spent adrift we'd known each other for three years and built a friendship based on a shared disdain for the world at large. Desmond was introverted and intellectual by nature; he preferred books and movies to interacting with real people, and so he usually avoided trouble. I admired his insight and was amused by his eternal cynicism.

Desmond in turn respected my philosophical discourse and my willingness to take risks.

"You can just leave if you want. You don't need to stay for this shit," Desmond said, offering me an easy out.

I shook my head. No way I was gonna bail on my friend.

"I'll stay and help out however I can."

Desmond nodded, visibly thankful for that answer, albeit in his reserved way. This was not a situation anyone cared to deal with alone. He went to the front door and opened it, letting the daylight flood in as the siren loomed louder.

2

Desmond and I walked down the road towards an empty lot where two old fireworks kiosks rotted away. After we'd told the cops what had happened they asked where Cole was. Desmond said he was probably holed up in one of the kiosks that he had claimed as a clubhouse. The cops then surprised the shit out of me when they suggested Desmond and I be the ones to go get him. In retrospect it was a smart call on their part. It avoided further confrontation, and the small .410 shotgun Cole had used to do the deed was lying on the lawn, so no danger there. Gerald had gifted it to Cole for his eleventh birthday just two months before.

Giving a gun to the child of the woman he abused probably wasn't Gerald's brightest move, but it would certainly be his last. He would die in the ambulance on the way to the hospital.

At the time, the ambulance hadn't even arrived yet, but we both figured Gerald to be a goner anyway. The mystery to me was how Desmond was taking all of this. He'd never been exactly chummy with his little brother. He was a half brother and lived mostly with his dad over in El Reno. Every time I ever saw Cole around he pretty much avoided Desmond unless he wanted to irritate him. If he did manage to annoy his older brother then Desmond was usually glad for the opportunity to punch the twerp. I'd never had a brother of my own, but from what I'd seen that's how a lot of brothers express their affection for each other.

We hoofed it across the littered lot toward the nearest kiosk. You could still see the faded epithet "Fireworks!" blasted across the front of it in what were once bright colors.

"You sure Cole's down here?"

"Yeah, pretty sure. He likes to play down here for some stupid reason."

We reached the intersection and walked to the closest kiosk's side door. Desmond put his ear to the door and listened a moment. He looked at me and nodded, then turned back to the door.

"It's Desmond, Cole. I'm coming in."

The door opened out. Desmond and I peered in to see his chubby round eyed brother sitting on the floor crying. Cole looked up at his brother and spoke in an unsteady voice.

"Is he dead?"

Desmond answered wryly, "Not yet. He'll be lucky if they can fit his fat ass into the ambulance."

Cole laughed despite himself. The laughter mixed with the tears, making him blubber. Desmond stepped in and put an awkward yet gentle hand on his head.

"C'mon, we gotta go."

Cole nodded and got it together. He stood up and met his brother's eyes. Desmond had a new respect for him. He'd had the balls to do what Desmond himself did not, and Desmond was just beginning to struggle with that fact. It was a struggle that would climax in the next few days, shedding new light in the darkness of Desmond's person.

Desmond turned to exit, and Cole followed suit. They stepped into the sunlight, and we all started the walk back up to the trailer house. As we walked, I tried to give Cole a pep talk.

"It's gonna be okay, Cole. You're just a kid. You were protecting your mamma so you're gonna be fine."

I decided to extrapolate on the particulars of his probable legal situation, at least as far as I saw it. Considering my experience, I wasn't exactly unqualified.

"Just so you know, they're gonna send you to juvie for a little while. You probably won't have to be in there that long. Just tell 'em you were protecting your mamma and that you didn't mean to kill him, and you might even get off scot free."

"And never believe the state appointed psychiatrist is your friend," was Desmond's bit of brotherly council. I later found out he'd stolen the line from that font of wisdom Jack Handey.

"Which basically means, just tell them what they want to hear and get the fuck outta there," I added at the time, trying to keep our advice digestible.

Well meant as our instruction was, it looked like Cole was too bewildered to absorb much of what we said. He walked with his head down and gave no indication he'd even heard us say anything. Desmond and I gave up on the pep talk, and all three of us walked the rest of the way back in silence.

3

Sylvia pulled herself together when she saw Cole and managed to answer the officers politely delivered questions in stride. They did not attempt to question Cole, but simply read him his Miranda rights, explaining to Sylvia it'd be best if he didn't say anything at this point. She agreed and so Cole sat next to her in a daze. To this day I have never seen police officers treat any two people more gently. Even when the reports were completed, and Sylvia wanted to ride with Cole in the back of the cruiser, they did not object nor was Cole handcuffed.

As they drove away Sylvia waved to Desmond, who stood on the front porch with me leaning in the doorway behind him. He gave a melancholy wave back, and stood lost in thought well after the car had disappeared down the road.

I broke the silence.

"You wanna get out of here for a little while? I could use some food." I was in fact hungry as hell, and I had a pocket full of cash.

For the usually home bodied Desmond, that sounded like a good idea for once.

"Hell yeah," he said, "Let's go."

It would turn out to be a fateful decision for both of us. I've often wondered if we had stayed put and cleaned up the mess like decent folks should whether the events that happened after would've ever transpired. Some of them likely would have occurred regardless, but others could have been avoided. Either way, it was time for some serious growing pains.

CHAPTER 3

After buying gas and bad food at the Texaco I'd robbed just a couple days before, Desmond and I cruised over to the dirtiest trailer park in the Flats where I spent an abundance of my time. I saw the usual crew of fellas hanging out in our regular spot, so I pulled up and parked.
As soon as we stepped out of the car I could hear Barry bitching about Hollister.

"What really pisses me off is that he hooked up Kirby's stupid ass. I can turn over twice the amount of product that shithead can."

His younger and much meeker brother Cass sat a few feet away, chugging a beer, paying little mind to his brother's seemingly endless series of drug induced monologues. They both occupied the front yard of Aaron, a strangely ageless looking burnout, who sat on his front steps craving the shot of crank he reckoned Barry probably had but wasn't in the mood to share just yet. He stared intently at the traffic going through a nearby intersection and offered Barry his support.

"Yeah, Kirby's his bitch for sure. I bet Hollister even makes him put a god damn dress on."

Barry smirked, spat a wad of phlegm, and took a drag off his smoke, unmoved by Aaron's wit.

"You'd probably like to watch 'em ya sick fucker."

Cass laughed aloud and joined in.

"That'd be a helluva sight, Aaron peaking in Hollister's windows." He laughed again and stood up to stretch his legs, particularly his left, which had been broken last year after Barry purposely ran him over in their driveway with his mom's car. Despite this and other incidents he still looked up to his unpredictable big brother. The rundown two bedroom trailer they shared with their terminally alcoholic parents was just a few blocks away. Fortunately Barry was rarely home. When he was he would generally just sleep for a day, sometimes two, eat whatever he could find, and then leave again.

Their attention turned to us. Barry eyed Desmond. It wasn't often they saw him out and about.

"What's up Dez? What are you doing in the land of the dead?"

Desmond and I said nothing, only exchanged a look at Barry's choice of words. He took note of our somber state.

"What the hell's going on with you two?"

Desmond shook his head then nodded to me, deferring to speak. I returned the nod and met the expectant gazes of the rest of the crew.

"Gerald's dead. Desmond's little brother Cole shot him this morning 'cause he was beating his mamma."

Barry and co.'s demeanors appropriately shifted. Feet shuffled.

"Son of a bitch," said Cass and nervously took a swig. Aaron whistled through closed teeth before having a realization.

"That's what all the sirens were about this morning."

Barry chimed in with his appraisal.

"Holy shit. Well, good for Cole." He looked at Desmond. "Your little brother's got some balls, huh?"

Desmond lit a cigarette and said, "At least one of us does." He walked a few steps away, staring at the traffic on the street. The others pretended to examine the treetops or observe traffic from another direction. None of them judged Desmond too harshly, for they all knew him to be the bookish sort, and most of them considered him smarter than themselves at any rate.

Barry looked to me, "You wanna do a blast? I got some of the good shit."

The monkey on my back howled, then somehow simultaneously grabbed my balls and kicked me in back of the head.

"I was hoping you'd say something like that. I could use a mood changer," said I.

Aaron licked his lips in anticipation, hoping he'd be included. He spoke up.

"We can go inside, but we'll have to give Janie a little if we do."

He wasn't telling Barry anything he didn't already know.

"We'll give her your shot. Let's go," he joked. Aaron's face twisted in shock.

"Fuck that, dude."

Barry laughed and stepped past Aaron, opening the door and heading inside. Aaron came close behind with Cass following after. I headed in and looked back at Desmond.

"You coming in, man?" I said.

Desmond turned, his eyes reflecting unhealthy thoughts.

"Sure," he said without much enthusiasm. "I could use a mood changer too."

2

The interior of Aaron's entire house was similar to Desmond's room. Blankets and tin foil covered the windows to block out all sunlight, although for different reasons than Desmond's, who shunned the sunlight because he kept odd hours, whereas Aaron was a paranoid addict who didn't want anyone seeing what happened within his walls.

Barry and I stood at the kitchen counter. Desmond watched from the side, while Cass sat in the adjacent living room with Janie, a crazy looking redhead who had lived with Aaron for the past ten years in a peculiar relationship based on codependence and mutual addiction. They rarely ever spoke to each other anymore except for such pleasantries as, "Don't bogart that joint" or "I fucked your friend last night." They had perhaps once loved each other, but the degradation inherent in their lifestyle had eroded that affection into an uneasy living situation that was becoming increasingly violent.

A couple months ago Barry bet me that it would be Janie who snapped first and put Aaron in the hospital. I foolishly took the bet and lost it just one week later in one of the most bizarre scenes I've ever beheld. Out of the blue Janie stormed out of the front door while we were all outside and threw a kitchen knife at Aaron. It zipped straight through the air like a missile and went right into

Aaron's mouth. Everyone freaked out. Aaron gagged in horror and spat the blade to the ground. What seemed like a fountain of blood issued from his mouth. I wound up driving him to the hospital. Apparently the blade only hit the back of his throat, and miraculously missed his teeth and his uvula. I never even bothered to ask what Janie had been so pissed about. Like today's adventure with Gerald I blew it off as just another day in the Flats.

Presently, Janie closely watched Barry as he gathered tools we were all familiar with. He first grabbed a big spoon from the sink and wiped it off on his pants. He then produced a small plastic zip lock baggie containing a yellowish white substance the consistency of kosher salt. He opened the baggie and dumped the entire contents, about a gram, onto the spoon.

"Since it's a special occasion we'll just mix up the whole damn bag. We should get 15 to 20 units a piece of some good thick shit."

Aaron appeared from the back room carrying a package of U-100 ultra fine insulin syringes. Dirty as his house was, he usually kept a stash of clean points just for such occasions. AIDS scared the shit out of most redneck junkies for two reasons. Reason number one is that you died. Reason number two is that you'd be branded a faggot before you died. We didn't fuck around with sharing needles. Besides, at the time you could just walk into almost any pharmacy and buy them outright. If they ever asked what they were for, you just said you were getting them for a diabetic relative.

Aaron passed Cass and an expectant Janie and placed the needles in front of Barry, who speedily fished one out and popped the top.

Desmond approached, eyeing the syringes strangely. I immediately knew he was thinking about doing a shot with the rest of us. While he'd always enjoyed pot and whiskey, he didn't really mess with the hard stuff except for the occasional line I gave him to snort.

"I know this isn't your thing Dez. We can chalk you up a little line since you don't shoot, huh Barry?"

Barry gave an annoyed look. He'd been shooting up so long he thought snorting it was a waste, but under the circumstances he was willing to make an exception for Desmond.

"Sure. He can chalk up a line." He started to take some the crank off the spoon when Desmond spoke up.

"I can shoot it too. Whatever," he said.

Barry and I looked at each other. Barry smiled. I did not. I looked hard at Desmond.

"Just snort a line and you'll be good."

Desmond wasn't in the mood to be patronized.

"It's no big deal."

Now Barry's gaze dug into Desmond with all of its intense fire. He spoke to him sincerely but not with a warning. I knew him well enough to see it was a challenge.

"It's a fuckin' Lay's potato chip. Once you do it this way, you'll never stop."

Desmond's eyes lit up. He took the bait.

"Well hell, now I really want to try it."

I wasn't into this, partly for Desmond's sake but also for my own selfish reasons. I had first introduced him to the drug. I didn't want to be responsible for creating another needle freak; partly due to my own lingering humanity and partly because my monkey didn't like to share, but also because Desmond was the only remotely grounding force in my life, a friend outside the circle of craziness I usually spun around in. I didn't want him to enter that ring.

"He's right, ya know. You should just do a line or not do any at all."

I motioned to the package of syringes.

"This ain't you, man."

Barry rolled his eyes, not caring for my sudden bout of conscience.

"Fuck it. If he wants to run with the big dogs let him try it."

Barry scooped the dumped crank back onto the spoon with the rest. Desmond picked up the syringe and held it out to him.

"Load it up."

I snatched the point out of Desmond's hand and got in his face.

"You better just chill out and hear what's being said. I'm trying to do you a god damn favor. The last thing we need around here is another vein to feed."

Desmond wasn't listening. It was a matter of pride to him now. If he backed down he'd feel like he wimped out again. He was unable to see at the moment that wimping out was exactly what he was doing. And to make matters worse, he obviously didn't believe meth was addictive enough for him to pursue it beyond the present moment. He pushed me away, angered by the violation of his personal space.

"I don't need any favors. Save the sermon for someone who gives a shit."

He reached over and picked up another one of the syringes. He pulled the top off and offered it to Barry, who sat grinning, enjoying the show. Desmond held out the needle.

"Load. It. Up."

Barry took it with a nod, appreciating Desmond's mettle.

"Your funeral," he said good naturedly. "Someone want to get me some water?"

Aaron, who watched impatiently for the drama to end, rose fast, went to the sink, and ran some water into a considerably less than sparkling glass. He brought it to Barry, who chewed the cotton off the end of a cigarette filter. I stood chastised off to the side while Desmond watched Barry's movements carefully. Barry noticed his interest and decided to give Desmond a tutorial.

"I'm gonna make a big mother shot first then squirt it into separate rigs for everyone."

He shot water onto the powder and crushed the crank with the flat end of the syringe's plunger, mixing it until it is dissolved.

"You want to make sure and get it all mixed up real good, just like the sugar in your iced tea."

"You don't need to put a flame to it?" Desmond asked.

"Not with crank or coke, they break down on their own." Barry answered. He next took the cotton from the cigarette butt. He rolled it between his fingers into a small ball, explaining.

"Before you drop the cotton in, roll it around good so there's no loose fibers. If they get into the shot you'll get cotton fever and feel like unholy shit."

He dropped the cotton into the middle of the viscous sludge. Barry placed the end of the needle onto the cotton and answered Desmond's next question before he could ask.

"The reason for the cotton is it keeps the needle from hitting the metal and barbing, and it makes it easier to suck up the nectar. Still, when you place the needle you need to make sure the bevel on the end is flush with the spoon. A barbed tip makes it easier to miss the vein, not to mention it leaves more of a mark."

As he drew up the fluid, Cass entered from the living room, interrupting the process. He'd been drinking steadily, and it was starting to show.

"Hey Barry, did you save me a line of that? I want to do some too."

Cass should've known better than this, regardless of his buzz. Barry only occasionally offered Cass a line and never let him shoot up; probably for reasons similar to why I was so averse to seeing Desmond doing it.

Without looking up, Barry gave him a warning.

"Go sit the fuck down. You don't need any."

Cass unwisely retorted.

"That ain't fair, Barry. All you guys are gonna get high, even Desmond. "

Barry slowly and carefully set the rig down half drawn. He then turned suddenly, stepped to Cass and threw him to the trailer house wall with a banging sound that was becoming too familiar. To this day, when I hear on aluminum can being crushed, I think of trailer house scuffles.

Barry leaned into Cass and spoke in a low tone laced with menace.

"Take the rest of your twelve pack and go home. Now." He pointed to the door. "Get the fuck out."

Tears welled in Cass' eyes, an involuntary reaction he hated, but couldn't help. He knew Barry might hurt him badly if he objected, so he walked to the other room and grabbed his last beer. Janie gave him a sympathetic look as he turned, opened the front door, and exited. He left the door open and yelled at Barry from outside.

"Fuck you, Barry! That ain't no way for brothers to _ "

Slam. Barry banged the door closed, cutting Cass off in midsentence.

"Fucking drunken dumbass motherfucker's been acting a bigger fool than usual last couple days," he spewed as he turned back to the half filled rig waiting on the countertop. Punishing Cass for his stupidity was routine for him, and he was already over it. He finished drawing the fluid into the mother shot then grabbed an empty syringe from the pile. He pulled the plunger out of the empty rig and shot about five units into it from the mother. He sat the mother down and held the newly filled rig vertically up to the light and flicked the body with his finger to get the air bubbles to rise to the top. He looked at Desmond.

"And if you shoot air into your veins you'll die, so be sure to prime the point."

Desmond watched as the air bubbles rose and formed into one. Barry gently pushed the plunger till the air bubble disappeared and a small bead of fluid bloomed at the needle's tip.

Barry held the rig out to Desmond. I watched with a painful mix of frustration and my own longing for the drug as Desmond took it with a dreamy, distant look in his eyes.

3

Twenty minutes later Desmond sat on the floor in Aaron's living room, staring intently at nothing as his brain tried to deal with what he had done to it. Sweat decorated his face and darkened his underarms. I knew full well how his heart trip hammered in his chest, and how the fire that raged in his head kept him from noticing. He'd never felt this awake before. Pure adrenaline coursed unnaturally through him, triggering parts of the mind reserved for extreme survival situations; like when you're trying not to be eaten by something.

Aaron stood a couple of feet away in the small living room. He had the stereo cranked up as much as he was and played air guitar to the heavy metal music braying from its speakers.

Janie sat on the other side of him in a chair staring blankly at some show on a 13 inch television screen while she incessantly rubbed her left elbow, which was close to bleeding from a barely healed scab. She bared several other marks from this nasty habit of absently wearing down her flesh in select locations on her body. I shuddered to think of the scabs I couldn't see.

Barry and I stood at the counter playing gin. We drew, rearranged, and discarded our cards almost frantically while Barry rambled about his favorite subject.

"And when I see Hollister the fucker better give me a good hook me up again, or I'll just take his shit, and then I'll go take Kirby's. Nobody's slinging dope in my neighborhood without cutting me in. Fuckin' Hollister even tried to tell me I was doing too much. Fuckin' hypocrite motherfucker. My problem ain't that I do too much. My problem is I ain't got enough. I'm a dedicated true blue motherfucker, and I ain't stopping till the day I die, and if any of those cocksuckers want to test me then they're gonna find out the difference between talking shit and walking it."

Lost in my own headspin, I was paying little attention to his diatribe. I'd heard this a million times. At first I didn't really get why Barry was so focused on Hollister. He could get dope elsewhere. However, after spending quality time with my volatile friend I understood it was about pride. Barry didn't like being told 'no'. Period. Especially from someone who had been a friend since childhood.

I'd met Hollister on a couple occasions and wondered if he really knew how dangerous Barry had grown. I hadn't known him nearly as long, and I'd seen first hand just how far his mean streak could go. One night while we were cruising the city, scoping out places for a potential score and not finding anything promising, a frustrated Barry grabbed a man off the street, beat him unconscious, and took his wallet, which had all of twenty dollars in it. I didn't like doing things that way. Mostly however, our working relationship was mutually beneficial. I supplied brains and a cool head. Barry supplied muscle and the ability to score decent dope from multiple sources at any time for a better than average price.

Barry interrupted everyone's shared desolation by bellowing at Janie.

"God damn it woman, stop picking your skin off. What the fuck is wrong with you?"
Janie came to, saw she was bleeding, and left the room in a rush. Aaron didn't seem to mind and went about changing the tape on his stereo while Desmond tried to process what just happened.

My mind returned to the game of gin I was playing with Barry. I finally picked the card I'd been waiting for. I slapped my hand down on the counter, making everyone jump a second time.

"Gin, bitch!" I said in triumph. Barry looked briefly at my winning hand before apathetically tossing his cards on the table. He wasn't much of a competitor at games unless they were the real life kind. He looked at Desmond and smiled a Cheshire grin, deciding on a new form of entertainment.

"Look at this guy," he said to no one in particular.
"Hey Dez, how you doing, man?"
Desmond answered without breaking his stare.
"I'm fuckin' fucked up," he said.
"Welcome to the club." Barry replied. He turned the grin toward me, and I knew it meant trouble.
"What are you thinking?" I said.

"Maybe we should take Dez on a run with us."

I'd always suspected Barry was genuinely crazy.

"Are you serious?" I said.

"Serious as a heart attack," Barry answered, confirming my suspicions.

"No fucking way," I said. Desmond would be a liability. He was a home body who knew more about the world of elves, orcs, and dwarves than he did about real life breaking and entering. For some reason Barry wanted to take him along, the gleam in his eye was clear on that, but I couldn't figure out why just yet.

"I don't think it's a good idea. He's never done anything like this before, and it's another person to split the take with," I said in a low tone, taking no chances on Desmond hearing anything over Aaron's music.

Barry eyed me facetiously.

"What's the matter? You afraid I'm gonna steal your girlfriend?"

My face flushed red. I was as homophobic as a Baptist minister at a drag show. I wasn't taking that kind of talk from anyone, not even Barry.

"That ain't funny, and if you want to throw down we can go outside right now."

Barry laughed at my sudden fire and held his hands palms up.

"Okay, calm down, spunky. I was just fucking with ya. What I really want to know is, what do you think you're trying to protect him from? He wants to prove himself. Let him decide, then back him up if he's your bro."

He had a point that was hard for a young man to argue with, but deep down I still didn't want to initiate

Desmond into this life. I looked at him where he sat spinning in the corner and thought he looked a lot like Cole did when we found him earlier that day. I sighed and turned to Barry, looking at him squarely.

"If he wants to go that's his choice, but if he acts a fool then he's walking home."

Barry nodded and grinned. In his own twisted way, he honestly thought he was doing Desmond a favor.

"He'll be just fine. We all will."

The feeling in my gut said otherwise, but I kept it to myself even as I watched Barry approach Desmond to see if he was up for a little action.

4

The three of us cruised through the Flats. It was an odd neighborhood that seemed purposely placed between the two towns of Guthrie and Edmond, as if neither wished to claim it as their own. Originally it was a community of oil field workers, placed there in the seventies to harvest black gold, but with the end of the boom came a lingering poverty. Likely bedfellows accompanied that poverty; alcoholism, domestic abuse, fatherless children, and now methamphetamines ravaged the mental and moral fiber even further. Only about two thousand people now lived amongst its gravel roads, trailer parks, and dilapidated homes, none of them untouched by these abuses. Those young people who were fortunate enough to avoid the pitfalls and stay in school left the first chance they got and never looked back. The rest stayed behind to have babies and collect welfare. A few worked thankless jobs or became cranksters like Barry and me.

I always laughed when I heard some ignorant fuck spout off about how lazy poor people are. The fact is that it's damn hard to work your way out of it. So hard that it's easier to just be poor. Nobody had the right to judge me or Barry or any of our friends. If it was even reasonably possible to actually work your way out of places like the Flats then people would gladly do it. Society wasn't providing any real answers, so we searched for our own, on our own terms.

Strangely enough, just as I settled into this conclusion, Desmond piped up and gave us an idea for our next score.

It was an idea that Barry and I couldn't resist.

5

The church lay silent as the mice that presumably scurried inside its walls. I shined my flashlight through a basement window and peered into an office. My light fell on a large picture of Jesus that hung on the wall over a desk. His benevolent face looked out peacefully yet somehow mournfully. His palms were held out to display their scars, proof of his suffering and divine mission.

I punched the glass of the small window. It exploded inward. Some of the shards flew across the room, hitting the picture and further scarring the countenance of our Lord before falling onto the desk and floor.

I scurried down the block to where Barry and Desmond waited in the shadows. No alarms sounded, and after ten minutes no cops appeared. When we felt safe and satisfied we put on our gloves and slinked back to the window. Barry cleared the broken glass from the sill and lowered himself down into the office.

I scrutinized Desmond, who stood wide eyed to the side, still ripe with the effects of the unfamiliar drug. He felt my sardonic eyes on him.

"What?' he asked annoyed. I imagined I could see the meth in his veins transforming his shame into a cancer; a malignant tumor that was goading him into doing things he usually had the wisdom to avoid.

"You want to stay out here and keep an eye out? That'd be best since we got three people," I said. I felt like I already had one unpredictable person to deal with in Barry and having two was more than I cared to deal with. Desmond, however, did not see it as a business decision and took it quite personally.

"Go fuck yourself, Todd. I'm going in." He hunkered down to lower himself in.

"What are you gonna do if the cops show up?" I asked him, wondering if he'd thought any of this through or not.

Desmond stopped, thought for a sec, and sarcastically busted out with, "Kick 'em in the balls and run like hell."

"Uh huh," I said flatly. "That's a great idea."

Desmond looked angrily up at me.

"Who are you to say shit about anything you fucking white trash junkie? How many times have you got busted? Is it 5 times or 6?"

I was nonplussed by this barrage. I knew who I was and where I presently stood.

"What are you trying to prove?" I asked, more curious to know if my friend was anywhere as self aware as I thought myself to be.

Desmond was saved from the question by Barry, whose face suddenly appeared in the window.

"What the fuck are ya'll doing out here? Get inside before someone sees your dumb asses."

Our argument was dissolved by the practicality of Barry's statement. Desmond lowered himself down, and I followed after.

Once inside, my eyes involuntarily went to the painting of Jesus while Barry and Desmond rifled through everything that opened. Desmond got lucky fast and found a fat zippered pouch in a bottom desk drawer.

"I think I found something," he said. He unzipped it and sure enough, a wad of bills resided inside. Barry swooped to his side for an appraisal. He snatched the pouch from Desmond's hands and pulled the wad out to reveal mostly ones.

"Whole lot of George Washington's in there. Let's see what other goodies we can find." He put the wad into his pocket and exited with Desmond following, perturbed that Barry took the cash from him but thankfully smart enough not to say anything about it.

I still stared at the picture on the wall with a faint smile on my lips. Although I was raised religious I didn't really have any moral issues with what we were doing. It was well outside our neighborhood, and I didn't believe churches helped anybody but politicians. Hell, even the parishioners looked like they were dressed to run for office. Where were the poor huddled masses and the sharing of food Christ embraced? I had stood in food lines with my mom on many occasions and often wondered why the Churches gave money to food banks but never shared food during services on Sunday. After all, that's what Christ did. He didn't direct people behind some building or down some obscure side street. He fed folks in the open where they worshipped, while raising public awareness and seeing to their health. I remember thinking even then that those were things folks could still do if they really wanted to, but the sorry truth was that the people that funded the churches didn't want to mingle with those poor huddled masses at all. I had attended services with my mom and grandma when I was a kid, and had always felt shunned by the better to do's of the flock.

I frowned, my smile lost in unwanted memories. All too often I found myself dwelling on the injustices of the world. It fed my addiction and provided validation for all of my actions.

I exited the room and turned opposite the way Desmond and Barry had gone, looking for things of value.

All in all, the score would turn out to be a good one in spite of my earlier foreboding about bringing Desmond. In addition to roughly two hundred in cash, we wound up with two laptops and a nice small stereo. The good vibes that came from the successful raid even restored harmony with me and Desmond.

Those good vibes would last through most of the evening. We drove to Oklahoma City and scored an eight ball from a guy at the airport that Barry knew. Then we drove to a twenty four hour pool hall where we locked ourselves in the bathroom and shot up. After that, Barry produced his seemingly never ending supply of small plastic baggies, so we could make a few quarter papers to sell to the other patrons. After a couple hours we made a good portion of our money back.

As we cruised back to the Flats, I again pondered my earlier anxieties about including Desmond. I told myself I had been paranoid and that Desmond had done just fine.

I almost shared my thoughts out loud, but I stopped myself. This ride wasn't over yet. I'd see how he was doing in a couple more days.

CHAPTER 4

The soft flesh surrounding the syringe's needle was pushed in and out like a trampoline as the rig was moved back and forth in jerky motions. Blood mingled with the amber colored fluid in the chamber. The jerking motions became more intense, back and forth, back and forth in futility.

Aaron watched in horror.

"You're fucked up, dude."

Even though I knew Desmond wasn't feeling any pain, I also grimaced at the scene before me.

"You're just rolling it on top of the vein. Pull it out and start over."

Barry smirked from the other end of the counter as Desmond tried to hit himself. Barry had done him the courtesy of injecting him the first time, but that was your only freebie when you hung with us. You had to learn to hit yourself if you wanted to play with needles. I'd thought maybe Desmond might back off and decide he'd had enough, but of course he didn't.

I couldn't watch anymore, if he kept this up he'd break the needle off in his arm. I reached out to help.

"You're gonna break it. You're done," I told him.

"Back the fuck off of me," he spat. "I'll get it."

"You're too spun out." I replied.

"I said I'll get it!" he yelled. A trickle of blood rolled down his forearm from the hole he was tearing. Aaron walked away,

"I can't watch." He went to the living room.

Desmond put an unsteady thumb on the plunger. I slapped the shot out of his hand. It fell to the floor next to Barry, who bent down and picked it up as Desmond flew out of his seat.

"I said back the fuck off of me!" he screamed in my face, and then grabbed me by the shirt. He outweighed me by twenty pounds, but I'd been in way more scraps than he ever had. I took his arms and used his weight against him. I spun him around and into the closed front door. Aaron jumped up from his seat in the other room.

"Whoa! Hey you guys take that shit outside!" he hollered.

Desmond kicked at me with all his force. I speedily stepped back, avoiding its brunt. He came at me in a fury.

Barry stepped in. He grabbed Desmond by the face and pushed him against the counter, leaning him backwards. He held him there with one hand while the other put the point of the retrieved needle in his face.

"Shut the fuck up and hold still or I'll stick it in your eye," he said with the utmost conviction. Desmond chilled out, staring at the needle like the barrel of a loaded gun. Barry took Desmond's unmarked arm, saw a vein, placed the needle, and then expertly registered and pushed the shot home. Desmond instantly felt the front door effects of the shot and his eyes went glassy.

"Thanks, but I would've gotten it," he said with minimal coherence or appreciation.

"That's your last shot for this run, Cochise," returned Barry, tossing the spent rig onto the counter and fishing a cigarette from his pack.

"Man, that gives me the heebie jeebies seeing the needle get dug around like that," said Aaron as he picked the rig up, inspecting its bent needle.

"Like you ain't never done it," said Barry, lighting his smoke.

"I know. I know, but still…" Aaron replied, dropping the rig into the garbage.

I looked at Desmond in disgust but didn't engage him further, only watched him as the effects of the shot sunk in. He walked to the living room, got a butt from the ashtray, lit it and kicked back on the couch, his fingers tapping an erratic rhythm on the arm.

In the last day he'd gone into a mostly silent shell. Seeing him like this was really starting to bother me. It reminded me too much of my own darker hours. I knew all too well the level of fevered introversion Desmond now experienced. His inner demons had been stirred into a frenzy by the crack of the methamphetamine whip.

I reminded myself that I had to let Desmond go his own course. So I dismissed my hypocritical criticisms and went to the counter to rig up a shot. My own demons were demanding their due. I stared at the crystalline substance and not for the first time considered putting the spoon down, walking out the door, and never looking back. But these were all the friends that I had, and while the drugs wore down my soul I still got a perverse satisfaction from living in this dark underworld. This was all that I knew. My hands even did their job by themselves. They deftly went about their work oblivious to my doubts, and by the time the shot was ready my thoughts had shifted to other things.

A loud knock banged on the front door. Everyone tensed. Aaron pulled a curtain aside to peek out.

"It's Cass."

Everyone relaxed. Aaron unlocked and opened the door. We squinted at the afternoon light like insane miners suddenly brought up from the depths. Cass stumbled in bearing ragged gashes across his left cheek and on his abdomen.

"What the hell happened to you?" Aaron said as he gawked at the mark on Cass' face.

"Fucking Lauren tried to kill me with a goddamn fork." Cass sputtered as he stumbled inside. I instantly knew this would produce more trouble.

Barry jumped up and to his brother's side, already agitated with him.

"God damn it, Cass. I told you not to be hanging out with that crazy bitch. Did you kick her fucking ass?"

"I think I broke her nose, she ran away bloodier than me." he said, more concerned with impressing his brother than with what harm he'd done to Lauren.

"Was mom home?" was Barry's next question.

"No, she's still at work," Cass replied, moving to the living room where Desmond rose, offering him the ratty chair he'd been sitting in.

"Good deal. Tell her you fell out of a tree or something," was Barry's sagely advice. He returned to the counter where I was just finishing my shot.

"More domestic squabbles. Must be a disturbance in the force," I muttered as I drove my shot home.

Aaron leaned over Cass, surveying the damage.

"That looks pretty bad dude. You might need to go to the hospital."

Cass held back tears of pain and shame. He wouldn't cry in front of them if he could help it.

"You sure you broke her nose?" asked Barry.

"Pretty sure," replied Cass.

"Good," said Barry, "You're gonna have a nice little scar on your face," he added lightly, sounding almost proud of his brother. But deep down, he knew as well as I did that this would create more trouble. He just didn't want to think about it right now. Lauren was Kirby's cousin, and Kirby had become tighter with Hollister as Barry had grown more distant. Plus, there had already been bad blood between Kirby and Barry over the years.

Cass didn't want to think about that fact either. In need of a buzz, he sensed an opportunity for charity.

"You guys don't have a couple bucks for some beers do you? Mellissa's car is over at Al's; if she's working she'll sell to me."

Fresh from the effects of my shot, I absently dug into my pocket and pulled out a five.

"Here ya go, man," I said and looked around expectantly at my peers. Barry and Desmond felt the vibe and dug into their pockets. Desmond, unable to really focus his vision, produced a one, and Barry handed over a bundle of ones. Aaron simply walked away, producing nothing. Cass was very grateful for the generosity.

"Whoa, shit, thanks guys. I can get some smokes too. Fuckin' awesome." he stood up, putting the cash in his right front pocket.

"I'll be back in a few," he said, almost chipper. He went to the door, opened it and exited into the bright daylight that flooded in, making us cringe once more. The door closed, and the room resumed its cave like ambiance. Aaron shook his head in wonder.

"What's with the bitches in this neighborhood anyway?" he said, oblivious to his own stupidity.

"Hell if I know," answered Barry, equally oblivious.

I could offer guesses about the obstacles confronting male-female relations in the Flats, but I was too high to effectively communicate at the moment. Besides, conflict of that nature was too commonplace, and I was just one spun out junkie who had no vested interest in the many illusions of love.

I began to pace, and Desmond moved to an empty chair and turned on the TV, his hand shaking as he hit the button. Aaron went to the stereo. Barry leaned on the counter top smoking, his inner wheels spinning.

I saw the concentrated look on Barry's face. I instantly knew he would be ready to go soon. He liked to keep things rolling for days, and we were just starting day three. I also figured Desmond was no longer a welcome addition on any outings at this phase of our extended wakefulness. I would be right on both counts. Almost on cue, Barry got my attention.

"So what do you think?" A smile appeared.

"About what?" I returned, feeling the question was pretty god damn vague.

"How about you and me go for a little drive?"

"That's a grand idea," I answered, most definitely ready to get outside. I was amped and itching to get out of Aaron's claustrophobic space.

"Let's go," Barry straightened up off the counter and went for the door.

Aaron and Desmond saw us mobilizing. Aaron said, "Where you guys going?"

"None of your fucking business," Barry shot back casually, as he headed out.

I grinned at Aaron and Desmond, dropped them a friendly nod, and headed out as well.

2

"When you get to the intersection, hang a right," Barry said as he lit two cigarettes at once, and then handed one to me. Barry only did that when he had something particularly crazy up his sleeve. I came to an intersection.

"Where we going?" I asked.

"Hollister's." Barry replied.

I paused, looking at Barry, who stared forward not meeting my gaze. I hung a right and went about a quarter of a mile before the pavement turned to gravel. It had been a dry spring and pale dust billowed in a huge cloud from under the back of the car as it crackled over the surface.

"What are you up to, Barry?" I finally asked.

"You should get your gun."

I hit the brakes. The fog of whitish dirt enshrouded us as we halted in the middle of the road. I looked him straight in the eye. I knew the answer to my next question but asked anyway.

"Are you serious?"

Barry shrugged.

"Just in case," he said.

I was not in the mood for this.

"You got your piece on *you*?" I asked, even though I knew the answer to that as well.

Barry leaned forward and pulled out his compact nine millimeter from behind his back. As far as I knew he'd never killed anybody, but I certainly felt he was capable. In all honesty, I was also capable but for perhaps different reasons. I was not naturally inclined to violence and rarely instigated it, but I would certainly back my friends in almost any hard conflict. And my choice in friends was as dubious as I was.

I leaned over and reached up under my ashtray to where I had ripped the inner paneling away. I pulled out my .32 automatic pistol and tucked it in my waistband under my t-shirt.

"You're gonna be the death of me."

He smiled his Cheshire grin.

"Just keep a straight face no matter what crazy shit I say, and we should be just fine."

I examined his face. He was in a wily way for sure, but the look in his eyes wasn't murderous. He obviously had a plan, so I decided to trust my friend.

I put the car in drive and we cruised on. As for the possibility of shooting someone or being shot myself, I talked myself into writing it off as an unfortunate but sometimes necessary job hazard. It wasn't always easy being an outlaw.

3

Me and Barry pulled into a gravel covered, oil stained driveway. A big aluminum shed and a double wide trailer were decorated with a yard full of cars in various states of disrepair. This eye candy was further garnished with an ever rusting cornucopia of junk.

Sitting in old folding chairs at one end of the open bay doors of the shed were Hollister and Kirby. An old wash tub turned table lay between them and hosted a couple tools, an assortment of nuts and bolts, a cribbage board, cards, and a presumably loaded .357. They eyed us warily as we pulled in and parked.

Hollister stretched his tall gaunt frame, stuck his legs out and put his arms behind his head. I could see his lips move.

"Well, there goes the day," I imagined him drawling to Kirby, who had taken some poundings from Barry while they were in school. While a year a half in state prison had hardened him enough to feel he could take Barry on, the concerned look on his face said he was in no hurry to test the theory.

Barry and I got out. His eyes were full of mischief. He saw another folding chair rusting next to an old Buick. He walked over, picked it up, unfolded it, and set it down in front of a cynical looking Hollister and an anxious Kirby. I stood a few feet away and lit a cigarette.

Barry looked right at Hollister, his sharp green eyes alive with unnatural vitality.

"What's up, Holly?"

Hollister looked right back. There was no fear in his eyes.

"What the fuck do you want?" he asked point blank.

"Front me an eight ball," Barry replied as if asking to borrow a cup of sugar.

Hollister cocked his head and looked at Barry in a way that made me think of people at the zoo when they see a particularly amusing critter doing something cute. He then spoke to me, but his eyes never left Barry's.

"What's going on, Todd?"

I looked in Hollister's direction and tried to ignore the gun on the table.

"Not much," was my reply. Hollister smirked.

"Pull up a chair," he said.

I nodded and eased down onto a seemingly discarded transmission.

"Thanks," I returned.

"Don't mention it," Holly replied.

Barry didn't care for the banter.

"So you just gonna ignore what I said?" he said, pretending to be wounded rather than angered. Hollister's smirk reappeared.

"I heard what you said. I just can't believe the size of your brass balls. Why should I hook you up again?"

"You're hooking up this little prick," Barry answered, motioning to Kirby, who tensed, but said nothing.

"He always pays me. You don't. You take my shit, and I don't see you for a week, then you come back with half the cash expecting me to give you more."

Barry leaned forward.

"So fucking what. I can move three times more crank than he can. If I take liberties then that's my goddamn prerogative for being a top salesman."

"And it's my goddamn prerogative to tell you to fuck off. I ain't fronting you nothing, not even a quarter paper. Bring me some cash or collateral then we'll talk." Hollister's hand reached toward the table for his cards, but Barry was thinking about the gun. He reached out cat quick, grabbed Hollister's wrist, and jerked him forward so they were almost face to face.

"If you want to get stupid about it we'll get stupid. You'll either front it to me or I'll just take it."

Tension pressed against the space between my temples in a sudden surge. Hollister looked at Barry like he was crazy.

Kirby stared at the .357. A look of sad resolve came over his face. I thought he was going to reach for it. My heart fell into my shoes. I reached under my shirt and put my hand on my gun. I stopped breathing and my heart sledge hammered in my chest.

Hollister just glared at Barry. It looked like his inner wheels were spinning faster than a coked up hamster.

Barry broke the spell. He casually called over his shoulder.

"Hey, Todd," he said.

I answered without taking my eyes off Kirby.

"Yeah," I answered as casually as I could muster in return.

"If Kirby's dumb ass even looks at that gun again, blow his fucking dick off."

Kirby looked my way and our eyes locked. He saw where my hand was. Time chugged like a sick engine. If Kirby made a move, there was no doubt in my mind about what I had to do. I would have to shoot him.

"What's it gonna be, Holly?" Barry asked.

Hollister yanked his wrist away from Barry, who let go easily but stayed leaning forward, within easy reach. Hollister tore his eyes from Barry and looked at me with intense scrutiny.

"Shit, Barry, he ain't even got a gun," he said with full skepticism.

Barry smiled. He felt the momentum was in his favor.

"He'd kill you for a teener, Holly," he replied with the praising tone of someone remarking on the skills of a respected craftsman.

Hollister looked at me again. I calmly lifted up the front of my shirt to fully display my piece and let my eyes tell him the truth about how far I'd go if this came to a head. I could see Holly rethink his previous statement.

He leaned back in his chair and guffawed while his mind searched for a way out of this situation. He could tell Kirby wasn't going to be much help if the shit hit the fan, but he couldn't just give in to Barry's demands outright.

"I'll tell you what, Barry."

Holly leaned towards him.

"I think I'll make you a little deal."

"And what would that be?" Barry asked.

"You got your gun on you?" Holly returned.

Barry paused. He wasn't expecting that question.

"You know damn well that I do," he replied.

It was Holly's turn for a facetious smile.

"Give it to me, and I'll front you the eight ball."

Barry thought hard, turning the offer over in his mind. He reached behind him and pulled out his gun. With his eyes on Hollister he released the clip and let it fall to the ground. He then cocked the gun to release the shell that was already in the chamber. It flew into the air and landed in the dirt a couple feet away. He turned the gun around, holding it by the barrel and handed it to Hollister, who took it and put it into his own waistband. Hollister reached behind their makeshift table and manifested a small coffee can. He opened it and pulled out Barry's eight ball. He tossed it to him, then spoke slowly and intently.

"If you fail to pay me in full, they'll find half your body in Oklahoma County and the other half in Logan County."

Hollister paused for final emphasis.

"I ain't putting up with this shit anymore."

Hollister turned and grabbed his cards off the table while Barry absorbed the last piece of info with a bemused look on his face. Kirby and I relaxed a little, feeling the drama had passed for now. Hollister looked at Kirby.

"Was it my crib?" he asked. Kirby shrugged, barely remembering they were even playing cards to begin with. He nodded anyway and picked up his hand.

Barry rose. I followed suit. As we turned to go, he stopped and turned back to Hollister, saying,

"Who do you think you'd get to cut up my body? The only person around here crazy enough to do something like that is me."

He then walked away, waiting for no reply and getting none. He and I got into the car. I started it up, and we hastily exited the premises.

CHAPTER 5

Now it's time to double back, and talk about some of the things that happened to Desmond after I left him at Aaron's.

But of course pages like these must obviously come with a disclaimer, for while many of the pertinent details were personally relayed to the author and can be believed, they can only be believed as much you're willing to trust a junkie.

That disclaimer aside, from here on out I'll be chronicling some of the trials facing individuals relevant to the remainder of this tale. Desmond is up first, so let's get to it.

My friend sat staring blankly at a picture on Aaron's wall of Ozzy Osbourne, who according to the caption scrawled across the photo was 'barking at the moon'. Ozzy bared sharp fangs and blood trickled down his chin, but it was the intense, fevered look in his eyes that Desmond dwelt on. He'd seen eyes like that recently, not just on his own face, but on the faces of everyone around him.

Two such eyes, unknown to Desmond, now came closer to his side. Janie had left Aaron to his headphones, where he could stay transfixed for hours listening to everything from Judas Priest and Motley Crue, to Pink Floyd and Carlos Santana.

She had different ideas about entertainment and seeing Desmond alone had made her instantly festive. It was well known to Aaron's friends (and to Aaron as well) that Janie would try to fuck anything that moved as soon as Aaron was absent; many of them had taken her up on it. Now it was Desmond's turn to undergo yet another initiation into this circle of freaks.

She leaned toward his ear. He sat unaware in the ratty chair, transfixed on Ozzy.. She blew on his ear softly.

He spasmodically leapt from the chair, instantly alive.

"What the fuck?" he shouted, spinning to see her grinning countenance.

Janie suppressed her laughter and put a finger to her lips.

"Shhhh."

"That wasn't funny," said Desmond, unhappy about anyone sneaking up on him.

Janie moved into the chair and leaned back, eyeing Desmond coyly as she wet a finger and mimicked fingering herself. He stared back slack jawed. He didn't know what to make of that. This was outside his realm of experience. He'd never been laid before, and his mind doubted what his suddenly stirring loins already knew.

She smiled at him, revealing a complete set of teeth, a rare occurrence in the Flats for people over thirty.

"Aaron's in his room with his headphones on. He stays in there forever when he's high," she said.

"So what," Desmond managed, while his loins battled with his brains for mastery of his senses. He wasn't particularly attracted to her, but the completely uninhibited looks she gave him were doing the trick none the less. Janie thoroughly enjoyed and thus approached these situations with an uncompromising zeal, which had made it difficult for others to refuse her as well. Myself included.

Janie rose and walked to him. He backed against the wall. She put her hand on his chest and spoke slowly as she moved the hand gently down his body.

"So what that means is I'm going to put your cock in my mouth, and I'm going to suck you off. After that, you're going to fuck me as hard as you possibly can."

She let that sink in for a second before asking.

"Is that okay with you?"

Desmond froze, unable to answer the question. He unconsciously licked his lips.

"I'll take that as a yes," Janie said and then popped the button on his jeans.

Desmond stood there in disbelief as Janie went down on him. He wasn't really sure how to feel about this. He felt strangely violated, but the prospect of finally losing his virginity was a prize too great to deny.

When you were super high on crank it could take a lot of doing to get a hard on, but after the main sail is raised it stays raised until the ocean is crossed. Janie was well aware of this fact. She took him in her mouth and went to work, making his anxieties evaporate.

In spite of the pleasure his body was experiencing, Desmond's mind wandered. He found himself thinking about when he was younger and had a gotten a tape worm.

He'd been about Cole's age, and they lived with his mom and his stepdad, Jim, who was Cole's biological father. Nobody knew for months that Desmond had the parasite. At first everyone simply thought he was growing out of his baby fat when pudgy little Desmond began losing some weight. Later, when he complained of abdominal pain and diarrhea his stepdad forced him to drink a foul concoction that caused him to shit out the invading organism. He soon rounded out again from eating the low quality government commodities he and his peers consumed on the reservation near El Reno, Oklahoma where they lived.

Desmond had hated it there and was glad when his mom and Jim had split. Like many natives his age, he didn't care one drop of piss for learning about the ways of his ancestors. He didn't know what he cared about except for wishing he lived in another world far away from this one. After Sylvia went on a bender and Jim said he'd had enough of her drinking, she spat venom in his face and he slapped her, something he'd never done before and didn't care to ever do again. He chose to end the relationship. Custody of Cole was fairly split between them in a somber but agreeable meeting. Sylvia was one of the nicest people you'd ever meet when she was sober. She often said later that Jim was the best man she'd ever known and it had been her fault for the break. After she and Desmond left the reservation they moved to Guthrie where she waited tables in a greasy spoon, occasionally having brief and sometimes volatile relationships before she eventually met Gerald.

Desmond was pulled from memory lane by the light raking of Janie's teeth over the tip of his dick. It wasn't altogether unpleasant, but certainly an attention getter. He looked down at her, and the surrealism of the moment was almost too much for him. He began to lose his erection. Janie felt the sudden decrease in enthusiasm and made a game time adjustment. She slowed down and took long, deep strokes that soon whipped him back to stiff peak.

When he let out a soft moan and started pumping his hips she spat him out, afraid he might come too fast. She quickly slid her pants down over her skinny ass and pulled him on top of her. She guided him into her.

And so a freshly fellated Desmond did his duty and gave Janie the business with his pants around his ankles and a thin lair of fog rising on his glasses.

2

Aaron exited his room and entered the short hallway to his living room. An old blanket turned into a curtain hung between the two spaces. As he approached the curtain, Aaron heard Janie and Desmond. He stopped and listened, instantly knowing what was happening.

For years he had simply chose not to react to these situations, always walking away or even entering the room, getting what he needed, and then exiting without saying a word. Over the last six months that had begun to change. He often peaked through a crack in the curtain, sometimes just staring, sometimes masturbating. He and Janie had not had sex together in over a year and only twice in the preceding two years. She was only interested when she was high, Aaron was never interested when he was high, and they were always high together. It was a grievous error in their relationship for one of them to get high without the other. The penalty for such a treasonous act was often violent and always piercingly loud.

Aaron parted the curtain and looked into the room. He saw Desmond humping Janie with primal fervor. Her hands were up the back of his shirt, and her nails were dug into his flesh. Small pinpricks of fresh blood dotted his back.

At first Aaron didn't recognize the emotion that began to fill him. He honestly didn't feel much emotion at all anymore besides the anxiety of wondering when his monthly check would arrive and when he could get another veinload of crank.

It wasn't until he parted the curtain further and took a step that he realized he was angry. He raised a fist and prepared to grab Desmond.

If asked why he had become enraged now, after all this time, Aaron wouldn't have been able to explain why. On a personal level, it was ultimately caused by hatred for himself, but as far as why it took place at this time in particular was anybody's guess. My best guess was that it was what some scientists called "emergence". I became exposed to this theory via PBS, and it was some badass shit. Like the coordinated movements of bird flocks and fish schools, to weather patterns and cosmic upheavals, emergence is the way complex systems and patterns arise out of a pool of multiplicity.

There had already been at least two other violent domestic disputes in the Flats the past few days. In police circles it is well known that crimes indeed seem to happen in waves. If a domestic abuse happens, you can almost bet it will soon be followed by two or three more violent conflicts, same with burglaries and homicides. Emergence is alive and well within human consciousness. Whether it is crime or fast food lines or customer service phone calls, people move and act in waves of motion that we do not often detect, and they can take us on a ride we do not completely control. Aaron was perhaps more susceptible than most to this effect, no doubt due to the suffocation of his willpower by the draining hobbies he was driven to take part in.

He grabbed Desmond by the shoulder and pulled him off of Janie with his left hand and brought his right fist down onto *her* face. That's right. He hit Janie, not Desmond. He hit her on the jaw, and her head snapped back from the blow, but she was not knocked out. Her hands flew instinctively up in the air protecting her. Janie had three older brothers. She knew how to take a punch, and Aaron only outweighed her by ten pounds. On the occasions that their arguments became physical, she was most often the least scathed.

She became enraged, her eyes widening as her cheeks flushed red. Aaron tried to hold her down with his left hand to hit her again, but she lunged upward and hit him square on the nose. Now it was his head that rocked back. He swayed, cupping his nose as blood gushed from it.

Desmond reacted to seeing Aaron hit Janie by grabbing the first thing he saw that he could pick up. It was the small, 13 inch television.

He raised it above his head.

It was an action without caution, judgment, or any foresight. It was the kind of reaction he wished he'd had when Gerald hit his mother. Unfortunately this was a different situation and his actions probably weren't even necessary. Janie likely had the situation under control.

She in fact sat up to clock Aaron again when Desmond suddenly brought the TV down on the back of his head. It hit Aaron with a loud crack. He fell limp to the floor. The TV fell to the floor next to him, and the glass screen imploded. The chord came unplugged when Desmond raised it up, sparing them any sparks, but a strange smoke poured out of the unit nonetheless.

Janie gawked at Aaron's still body. It lay twisted into a morbid shape, reminiscent of the poses of ancient corpses that had been preserved by the engulfing ashes of a volcanic eruption.

Janie looked at Desmond with panic in her eyes. Desmond stared back, equally unhinged by this turn of events. He reached down and pulled up his pants.

"What are you doing?" Janie managed to ask before he turned to the door, yanked it open and left as fast as he could. The door remained open in his wake, and Janie shielded her eyes from the ensuing daylight.

Desmond's own eyes squinted against the sunlight, and he adjusted his glasses. He scurried across the street to Al's Short Stop, a small gas station at the corner of Waterloo and Coltrain where our crew often hung out.

Cass crouched in the alley between it and a vacant building. He sat a few feet in, out of the morning light, drinking a beer and smoking a cigarette with the rest of a sixer beside him.

"Hey, what's up Desmond?" he asked casually before seeing Desmond's sweaty panicked face.

"Wow, you look like shit," Cass remarked before adding, "Though I guess I ain't one to talk, huh?" He touched the fresh gashes on his face and took another swig of beer.

"I think I killed Aaron," said Desmond, making Cass almost spit up.

"What the fuck did you say?"

Desmond said it again, this time tasting the words in his mouth like slow poison.

"I think I killed Aaron."

Cass looked incredulously at Desmond, his mouth agape.

"Are you shitting me?" he asked with minimum skepticism.

Desmond shook his head, and his face contorted. Cass was stupefied but managed to make a profoundly obvious statement.

"You're having a hell of a time these days," he said then took another swig of brew. Desmond briefly considered strangling him before his already struggling ability to concentrate was broken by a piercing scream from across the street.

"YOU MOTHERFUCKER!"

Desmond and Cass looked to see Aaron standing in his doorway. He lurched down his steps like a zombie, blood covering his face and shirt from the blows he'd just sustained. Desmond was at once relieved and horrified at the sight of this undead creature. Aaron shambled across his lawn and into the street heedless of traffic. A car screeched to a halt in front of him, but he was completely oblivious.

"I'M GONNA FUCKING KILL YOUUUU!" he volleyed in that same primal scream, his eyes blazing as he glared at Desmond.

Desmond did not hesitate to act. He ran down the alley and into the neighborhood beyond. He'd had enough social interaction to last him a lifetime and had no wish to prove himself to Cass or Aaron or anyone else by staying to deal with this situation.

Aaron saw him take off and picked up the pace, but he was too impaired to gain any real speed. He stopped next to Cass and watched Desmond disappear around a distant corner. He slumped against the wall. Cass offered him a beer.

"Well I'm glad you're not dead," he said. Aaron took the beer and glared in the direction Desmond took off in.

"That motherfucker is going to be the next time I see him," he bluffed.

"What the hell happened?"

Aaron paused and looked around like a man in a dream. He had a severe concussion, and though it was oddly fortunate the artificial adrenaline in his system helped him stay conscious, he was loopy nonetheless. White spots swam in his vision while moving objects left tracers in the air.

"I don't know what happened. I don't know," he finally answered. Not usually a drinker of alcohol, he opened the beer and took a sip only to set it down and slowly get to his feet.

"I gotta go," he muttered then lurched away, meandering back across the street to his house.

Cass watched him go, finished his beer, and then grabbed the one Aaron left behind.

3

Desmond now walked along a roughly paved street with his mind still spinning. He'd only taken his last shot about an hour and a half ago. A good shot could keep a rookie like him going hard for twelve hours or more. Every site and sound penetrated his eyes and ears with a clarity so severe it impaired the senses rather than improving them. He stopped and did a 360, then took a deep breath. He looked around and tried to focus. He noticed a woman looking out of her window at him. The look on her face said she wondered whether he was crazy or not. He looked quickly away and walked on, wondering the same.

One of the rare and perhaps the only potential benefit of methamphetamines is that it can create introspection so intense it leads you to the bottom of your self. When you get there, you have to confront that self and accept it. If you achieve acceptance you'll still be high and may do dumb things, but you'll basically be functional. If you reject yourself then the drug keeps you locked in that introspective state until you find acceptance or you come down from your debilitating high. Either way, until one of those two things happens you'll morph into a twitchy lump on someone's couch that can barely speak.

As Desmond walked down the street he started to feel comfortable inside his skin again. The movement of his body kept him in it. His thoughts began to run more smoothly. He got his bearings and was glad to realize he was walking in the general direction of his house.

It was a two mile walk that would take him almost fourteen hours to complete.

CHAPTER 6

"I can't believe we got away with that shit. What would you have done if Kirby had just gone for that gun right away?" I asked.

Barry shrugged apathetically.

"You mean, what would *you* have done?" he returned.

I stared forward and pondered the question.

"I don't know. I don't know what I'd have done," I answered, but I knew what I would have done. I would have pulled my gun and shot Kirby in the face as fast as I possibly could. That fact frightened me more than the possibility of being shot myself.

"You got any points on you?" Barry asked, breaking my train of thought.

"Um. Yeah, check the glove box," I replied.

Barry popped the glove box open. He dug through empty cigarette packs and a torn up owners manual and found a couple of U-50's, smaller than the 100's but still usable.

"Awesome. Let's go by my house. No one is home, and I wanna cut this shit in half so we can do up some choice rocks for ourselves."

"Right on," I said enthusiastically. I knew this plan well. Take the purer dope, divide it in two, add powdered B-12 to one half and sell it at full price, then save the good shit to do yourself. It was a common procedure that often trickled down. Sometimes a batch of good dope would get cut in half by one person then cut in half again by the next buyer, and so on until some poor chump bought a quarter of dope that was almost all B-12, which turned your pee a bright yellow. There were quite a few less connected addicts in the Flats who had neon piss and a hard jones for a good fix. At least the junkies were getting their vitamins.

2

I sat on Barry's couch with my wheels spinning and quite literally thought about the meaning of life while Barry was in the back cutting the eight ball he'd scored from Hollister.

Why do they call it "The Meaning of Life" anyways, I wondered. That's some kind of bullshit. Life has no meaning till you decide on one. I thought they should call it "The Decision of Life" and make people take responsibility for themselves. Not that I was one to talk about responsibility.

I laughed aloud at that last thought, then stood up, stretched, and walked through the open front door to the small porch where I began to pace. I distinctly remember my next thought.

If it's up to me to decide for myself what life means then what's my choice?

There immediately seemed to be too many possibilities.

I mulled that over and walked back and forth across the porch. I was still high as hell, and when the mind waxes philosophical at high voltage the current jumps around. My scattered thoughts struggled to consider reasonable possibilities with which to fill my personal life bubble. I had the outlaw persona, as well as the occasional philosopher/social commentator, but I found myself wanting something deeper. I tried to think it through but just went in circles till I wound up where I started from, so I again pondered the meaning of life on the macrocosmic level instead of through the prism of my own choices.

I then had what was to me a scientific revelation. The meaning of life could be defined in a general scientific sense as 'the attempt by living creatures to overcome the confines of physical existence'. All creatures strove for food and comfort. Humans were only different in that we took this to other levels, but the same principle applied. It was just that we also attempted to overcome the confines of own minds. We strove for mental comfort in a dense jungle of competing ideas and self made goals. Either way, whether the attempt to overcome was physical or mental, conscious or unconscious, it could all be summed up in one word.

Growth.

That made me wonder whether all that Garden of Eden business that had been shoved down my throat was an analogy for the web of life and how we should better tend our gardens on the inside as well as the outside. That in turn made me think that death really was an illusion, like a seed pod that blindly encased you until it was time to be cast aside.

This last thought gave me the chills. I was spared further revelation by the sound of Barry tromping out from the back room. He walked onto the porch looking like a sweaty redneck grim reaper and lit a cigarette.

"You about ready to roll?" he croaked.

"For sure. I'm just wearing a path across your porch," I replied, and lit my own cigarette. We still had a few cartons of smokes left from our score at the Texaco, but we were burning through them mighty fast.

"Let's go down to the corner and hang out so we can turn some of this," said Barry, referring to the freshly cut stash we needed to sell.

"Right on to the right on," I said, still shaking off the remnants of my thoughts on life.

We made for the car and cruised across the Flats toward Al's, where we would find Cass caught up in a sudden world of shit. There was rarely a dull moment in the Flats.

3

Cass sat at the corner and drank his brews, watching the traffic go by, wishing someone he knew would swing by so he had some company.

He got his wish when Kirby pulled in his truck.

Cass recognized the vehicle, and he froze in mid swig. Lauren sat in the middle of the cab between cousin Kirby and her brother Ron. Two other bruisers, Lane and Mike, rode in the back. All of them looked at Cass with unhappy faces. Lauren's face was a purple mess.

Kirby had found out about the incident with Cass and Lauren just minutes after Barry and I had left Hollister's. In no mood for cards after almost getting into a gunfight, Kirby forfeited the game and cruised over to Ron's, where Lauren was recovering from Cass' blows.

Once the two men exchanged council they naturally told themselves this was legitimate cause to distribute a beat down. Cass had done stupid things before and been spared serious injury by the fact that he was Barry's brother, but this time his ass was grass. Kirby got Ron and Lauren into his truck then rounded up Lane and Mike.

He and Ron were both pleased and surprised to find Cass on the corner alone. They parked and all of them piled out of the truck. Cass stood up, not bothering with trying to run.   Lauren stood by the truck with eyes of vengeance while the four men approached Cass.

"Hey, Kirby. What's up?" asked Cass, trying to be brave. Kirby ignore his question and got right up in his face.

"You think it makes you a man to hit girls, motherfucker?" he spat. Cass backpedaled.

"What was I supposed to do? Look at my face, dude. She's fucking nuts," he replied. He was right about that. Lauren was a pretty little thing, but she was a hard drinker like Cass, and their relationship was as tumultuous as any in the Flats. However, Kirby and company were not sympathetic to the finer details of their love affair.

Kirby punched Cass in the face. He stumbled back. Kirby moved in and kicked him in the guts.

"You don't fuck with my family," he yelled. "All of you god damn losers that hang out on this corner need to get the fuck on down the road. Things are hard enough without your bullshit. Especially your brother's bullshit. He's walking a thin line."

Cass managed to reply, "Then you need to talk him about that."

"Believe me, I will," said Kirby. "Right now I'm talking to you."

Kirby stepped back and nodded to Ron to let him know it was his turn to take out some frustrations on Cass. Ron moved in and was about to deliver his own kick when Al walked out of the store.

Al was a large, mature black man who was treated with great respect, albeit of a peculiar variety. Since he was often referred to as 'that big ole nigger' he was obviously not regarded as an equal, but since he had the guts to own a business surrounded by crazy white people, he was treated courteously and rarely belittled to his face. Besides, Al didn't take shit off of anyone, and he often told us to get off of his property. He knew we were all high and selling crank, but his property line ended at the alley, so we'd just hang out there. As long as we maintained that little bit of distance he generally let us be, unless too many of us gathered or a fight broke out.

"You boys need to move on," Al boomed to the gang that loomed over Cass.

"We're just talking, Al," replied Kirby.

"Go talk somewhere else," volleyed Al. He didn't like calling the cops, but he damn well would. He'd rather have one cop car in his parking lot than three of them with an ambulance.

Unfortunately for Al, it wasn't his day.

Barry and I pulled up to the stop sign at the intersection and looked over to see Cass in the middle of his shit storm.

"Fuck," said Barry. "And I don't even have my gun."

"I got mine," I said, and then took a sharp turn to tear into the parking lot. I drove right at Kirby and his crew, making them scatter before I screeched to a stop. Before I even had the car in park Barry was out the door and yelling at Cass' assaulters to back the fuck up. They did no such thing, but held their ground.

"I'm calling the cops," hollered Al, and waddled back inside his store. No one paid him any heed. Ron gave Cass another kick to goad Barry into action. Lane, Mike, and Kirby spread out as Barry closed in with a full head of steam.

I got out of the car. I pulled my gun out and fired a shot into the air. Everyone jumped except Barry, who never broke stride. He decked Mike with a right and he went down. I pointed my gun at Kirby as I came closer.

"Get the fuck out of here unless you want your ass shot," I warned.

Kirby froze. Lane and Ron backed cautiously away. Mike scampered away from Barry. We all stood there looking at each other for a few seconds, then Cass got to his feet, grabbed Kirby from behind, and spun him around.

"Now what've you got say?" he mocked, then punched him in the gut. Kirby doubled over, and Barry moved in. Kirby's crew stood to the side, unsure what to do. Lauren had climbed into Kirby's truck and locked the door. She stared out wide eyed, watching the action.

I trained the gun on Lane, Ron, and Mike.

"Beat feet, motherfuckers. Get out of here. Now." I commanded. They paused, looking at Kirby, who was left standing between Cass and Barry.

I cocked the hammer back on my pistol.

"I said go."

They backed away but didn't fully retreat. Ron's eyes met with Lauren's, and I knew he wouldn't just abandon his sister.

Barry grabbed Kirby by the throat and backed him into a telephone pole.

"How's it going, Kirby? Long time no see," he cordially spouted before ramming the back of Kirby's head into the pole.

Kirby's eyes rolled over, and he dropped like a sack of dead puppies.

Al yelled out the front door of the store, "I called the cops. You better get the hell off my corner," he warned.

Barry turned to him and replied, "It's not your corner, dickhead. It's ours."

Al scowled and ducked back inside. Barry turned nonchalantly to me.

"You want to go or you want to hang out a while?" he quipped.

"I reckon we should go," I hastily answered. I knew Al wasn't bluffing about calling the cops, and it looked like Kirby might need an ambulance. His crew lingered on the other side of his truck. I kept my gun ready as we moved towards my car. Cass fell in behind.

"I'm going with you guys," he said. Barry turned to him.

"The fuck you are. Take your ass home."

Cass stopped, hurt by the exclusion.

"It's Todd's car," he said and looked hopefully at me.

This was annoying. I didn't want to be caught in the middle of any of their arguments. We just needed to go. Pronto.

"You'll be safer if you hoof it. We'll catch up with you later, man," I reasoned. Cass paused, unsure. Barry reiterated his position.

"Take off. I don't want you riding with us," he said with a stern look before opening the car door and plopping into the seat. I got in as well.

"Fucking bullshit," whined Cass. He gave us a sad look then took off down the alley.

I had no time to feel any sympathy. I fired up the engine and squealed out of the parking lot.

We circled back around Al's and headed into the heart of the Flats where side roads connected in a chaotic web that Barry knew like the back of his hand. We flew down the road about as fast as my old Chevy's sluggish V6 would allow.

I peeled hard around a corner. Barry grasped the door handle to keep from falling in my lap.

"Easy," he nervously advised.

"I got it," I returned, in no mood to have my driving questioned. Barry was in no way assured by my answer.

"Where the hell are you going?" he asked.

"Away," I replied in all honesty. I was simply putting distance between us and where the cops would soon be.

He gave me a funny look then offered a destination.

"Let's go to Blindman Bill's. Hang another right up here."

That was a good idea. Bill's place was tucked back in a weird cul de sac next to a pond. We'd be able to park out of sight and wait out the drama down on the corner. Or so we hoped. This wasn't the first time a gun had been pulled on the corner, and the unwritten rule in the Flats was to never tell the cops shit. The punishment for talking to the pigs was extreme. At best no one would ever trust you again. At worst you'd wind up dead. Such occurrences weren't common, but they were not unheard of either. We had to trust that Kirby and his crew wouldn't give them our names. I wondered briefly if Al might talk to them, but I reminded myself that Al knew the rules too, and to my knowledge he'd never filled out a police report or pressed charges on anyone despite his occasional calls for assistance.

As I turned down the windy back road that led to Blindman Bill's, I told myself everything would be okay. I couldn't have been more mistaken.

CHAPTER 7

Desmond walked down the road near the edge of the Flats. He came to an intersection where he could turn left or right, but not forward. He'd gone about a mile and had about a mile to go, plus or minus another half mile, depending on which way he now took.

He opted to jump the fence and cut a straight line across the next square mile. It was an area that would be the home of a future suburb, but at the time it was still covered with trees.

Desmond had been gone for three days now, and Sylvia would have been worried sick if she had been home, but she was on a bender with her consoling yet equally alcoholic friends. She had hardly been home herself since the shooting. As for Cole, he only had to stay in custody for a little over a day before he was released to his dad till the next hearing.

Safely over the fence, Desmond trudged off into the trees. In optimal conditions he could have made the trip in twenty minutes. The landscape was wooded but flat, with little underbrush to navigate around, so the path should have been easy. Unfortunately, Desmond brought along his own obstacles. When you're as high as he was you tend to see and hear things that aren't there. Every dusty ray of evening sunlight messed with his depth perception. Every soft chirp or snapped twig was amplified ten fold. He wasn't frightened by the sights and sounds, but combined with his swirling thoughts it sufficed to distract him enough to alter his course. Desmond was soon meandering haphazardly and totally unaware of it.

Knowing it would annoy him to no end, I would later liken his experience to a young Indian brave on a vision quest. I wasn't disappointed when he told my lily white ass to fuck off. He hated nothing more than the many ignorant caricatures of his people. In fact, for a time he hated them so much he even rejected his heritage altogether. He was a peculiar fellow to say the least.

As far as his current thoughts were concerned, they meandered as much as his person did. One second he was imagining Gerald bleeding on the floor, then a random scene from a movie, then a piece of cheese, a passage from a book, his brother, an old picture, a goat, French fries, his mother, Janie, the goat again, Kafka, Aaron screaming at him, and Regis Philbin, who was the last thing Desmond saw on Aaron's 13 inch TV screen before he grabbed it and clubbed Aaron over the head with it.

For almost two hours Desmond floated about in this state of subdued stupefaction, until he came into a small clearing and saw a thing of beauty that at once amazed him and boggled his mind.

It was a colossal full moon that seemed to fill half the sky.

He hadn't even noticed that the sun went down. Desmond looked around with wonder at the sudden presence of night. The theme song from The Addams Family sprung between his brows, and he smiled. He hummed along and gave himself the giggles. Then he got the giggles from his giggles and erupted in mad laughter so fierce it doubled him over onto the ground. After he exhausted all his breath, he lay there feeling cleansed after a great purging.

Desmond looked back up at the giant lantern disk in the heavens and basked in his smallness. It was an amazing, wonderful feeling, like the lifting of a thousand burdens. As far as he could remember, it was the first time he ever felt at peace.

He laid there in this euphoric state until he eventually drifted into an uneasy sleep filled with strange dreams and distorted memories. There he would remain almost till the dawn.

2

I slowly cruised past the grey Camaro in Bill's front yard, vaguely wondering who it belonged to, before I forgot all about it and pulled around back. As soon as I threw it in park, Barry and I hopped out like synchronized tweakers and made for the front door.

Barry knocked, and Bill answered from beyond.

"Who is it?" came his scratchy voice.

"The fuckin' Easter bunny," jibed Barry. I suppressed a laugh.

We heard light feet pitter patter to the door. I figured it must be the owner of the Camaro, probably some crankslut ole Bill had over for some satisfaction. And don't get me wrong by my use of the term "crankslut". I love me some sluts. In my honest opinion, if there's one thing the world needs more of, it's sluts. If every man got laid regular there'd be little or no war, and competition in general would be laissez faire at best. Combine that with an empowered female population and society might grow into something as close to a utopia as we can realistically get. That was my theory anyways.

My attitudes about love and sex in general were quite cavalier, but I at least knew the difference between the two. One I had occasional use for, the other I did not. To me love was nothing more than another chemical reaction in the brain, even more deadly than my usual alterations of consciousness. I had seen what love could destroy. Meth was safer. It numbed the heart and lit the mind on fire. I appreciated beauty for beauty without the need to possess it. Even when a pretty girl did manage to tug my heart chains, I wasn't fooled. I knew what the prick of a needle felt like. Why life tried to penetrate us with its own agenda was a frequent mystery to me. I often felt fortunate that I chose my own ways to be pricked, and love was not a drug of choice.

Then Bill's door opened, and I met the gaze of Vicki Atma.

God damn it.

My heart fell into a deep chasm. At first I thought it was despair that I was feeling, but then I saw the emotion for what it really was. I was totally flabbergasted and would have laughed in the face of anyone who said this could happen to me. Everything changed. I fell in love.

I know that all sounds stupid and cliché, but it's still the truth. I don't believe in Bigfoot, the Loch Ness Monster, or alien abductions, but I will forever be a believer in love at first sight because I experienced it firsthand.

Vicki's eyes never waivered from mine as she pulled the door wide and politely waived us in. Barry took no notice of our visual embrace. He sauntered inside and plopped down on the couch. I stepped in tentatively, unable to tear my eyes away from hers.

Finally, she looked away first and closed the door. With the spell broken I managed to walk to the couch and sit down next to Barry. I felt dazed.

Bill sat in his old La-Z-Boy chair. His perpetually dark sunglasses sat in their usual spot atop his nose. He told everyone that he lost his sight via an accidental explosion on a construction site, but rumors occasionally surfaced that this wasn't true and that he could actually see. I and none of my peers had ever witnessed anything to support this theory, but cranksters love a good conspiracy and strange gossip was a common occurrence.

"Who do you have there with you, Barry?" asked Bill.

"Hey there, old man," I said.

"Ah. Hello, Todd," he returned, recognizing my voice. I tried not to look at Vicki as she walked over and sat in the chair next to Bill. I was still trying to process what just happened.

"Boys, this is Vicki. You may remember her, Barry. She's Maria's half sister."

Barry looked her up and down. I suddenly felt yet another emotion on a level previously unsurpassed. Jealousy. God damn it again.

"Yeah, I remember," observed Barry. "It's not like there's a lot of good looking Mexican girls around. You moved to Seattle or something, right?" he asked, his eyes all over her. My whole body twitched. I calmed my irrational fears and told myself to get a grip.

"That's right," she replied. "Good memory."

Her voice was as dark and soothing as the rest of her. Barry reached into his pocket for his stash. He tossed the eight ball onto the coffee table.

"Well, welcome back to paradise. You wanna do a blast?"

She didn't seem impressed, but Bill's interest was piqued.

"Let's see what you've got," he said, with a touch of irony in his voice. He leaned forward, and his hand roamed the table top till it found the dope. He picked it up and felt the texture of the product through the bag. Next, he opened it up and took a good whiff of its fine fragrances. Satisfied with his examination he zipped it back up and gently placed it back onto the table.

"Check this out," he said with a sly smirk on his face. Now it was Barry's interest that was piqued as he watched Bill open up the drawer on the round lamp table that sat next to his chair. He pulled out a tray covered with what had to be about a quarter pound of the purest crystal either me or Barry had ever seen.

"Holy shit," said Barry.

Bill set the tray on the table, and we moved in for a closer look. Most of the meth we'd ever done was made by half assed, back woods chemists who often had mixed results with their products. Sometimes the shit was good, sometimes it wasn't. The stuff we were now drooling over was on a level we hadn't seen. If we ever got dope like this, it was after it had been chopped up and cut down, not in the pure unadulterated glory we now beheld on the tray before us.

"That ain't no bathtub crank," remarked Barry. "Did you cook this up, Bill?"

"I did indeed," he answered. Barry wasn't fooled.

"Bullshit," he spat. "Ain't no way anyone around here made this."

He gave Vicki a sly look. "You brought this back from Seattle, didn't you?"

Vicki eyed him carefully and smiled in a way that gave me chills. She was smooth.

"No. California," she replied, only the slightest bit annoyed that Barry so quickly figured out she was the real hook up. Bill was way more upset about it than she appeared to be.

"I'm sorry, dear. I didn't think – " he started.

"Don't worry about it," she interrupted. Bill relaxed a bit. Barry picked up a rock to take a closer look.

"Fucking A. Very nice. This shit looks deliciously deadly."

I nodded my agreement and chanced a look at Vicki. Our eyes locked once more.

"You have no idea," she said, and flashed her chilling smile again.

"So, you guys gonna let us try some or is this just show and tell?' inquired Barry.

Bill returned to host mode. "Oh, I think we can spare a taste." He grabbed the tray and sat back with it in his lap. His hands danced over the rocks. One picked up a gram sized chunk and held it out to Barry.

"See how this does you," he offered. Barry's face lit up like a Christmas tree.

"Hell fucking yeah."

He snagged the chunk from Bill's outstretched hand and set it on the table. He then quickly began unloading his tools to rig up a shot. He still had the two points I'd given him earlier, plus a spoon he'd grabbed from his house before we left.

"I got a clean point I can draw a mother load into if everybody wants to partake," he ceremoniously offered.

"Oh, I'm doing just fine at the moment," said Bill. "But thank you."

"Same here," added Vicki.

"More for me," assessed Barry.

I was still feeling pretty amped too. It had been a busy day. I was almost tempted to pass on a shot as well, but the kryptonite before me was too tempting to deny.

"I'm in," I said.

"Cool. You wanna grab some water?" asked Barry, without really asking.

"Sure," I said half heartedly and started to my feet. Vicki hopped up first.

"Here, I'll get it for you."

I watched her walk into the small open kitchen and fill a coffee cup with water. In the back of my mind I vaguely heard Bill talking to Barry.

"When you get done with that, do you think you might be up for a game of chess? I'm betting this is your night."

"Sounds like a sucker bet."

"The only sucker is the one who doesn't dare wager," replied Bill.

Vicki returned with the water and set it down in front of me.

"Thank you," I croaked, my voice suddenly betraying me.

Once again her chill smile spread its quiet wings across her beautifully haunted face, making my heart stop and my mind freeze. Fuck, I had it bad. I told myself there was no way this could turn out to be a good thing, but even that thought was a waste because it wouldn't deter me. This connection was too fierce, and I could tell by the look in her eyes that it was mutual. I knew we would soon be together, for good or bad.

CHAPTER 8

"Pawn to Rook 4," said Barry.

"That's a good move," returned Bill.

I stood in the doorway to Bill's small study and watched Barry get his ass whooped, which Bill did quite regularly to whomever he might be playing at the time. His nimble hand glided over the board and moved one of his knights.

"Check," he cordially informed Barry.

"Fucker," was the absent reply as my friend looked for a way out of Bill's trap. Sweat ran down his face, and his leg spastically bounced hastily up and down, but Barry wasn't nervous.   The primo vein candy we'd partaken of was merely taking its toll.

I too was a mass of barely contained convulsions. I grew bored waiting for Barry to decide on his next move, so I turned and headed back into the living room hoping for some time with Vicki. Finding the room vacant I made for the back porch.

There she was, sitting in a plastic chair under the light of the full moon smoking a cigarette. I tried to think of something to say, but couldn't manufacture a coherent thought. She saved me by speaking first.

"I love the quiet here. I didn't know I even missed it until I got back. It's almost mystifying to me now."

I listened to the quiet spring night. In the late summer the cicadas would be buzzing, along with the crickets and the frogs, but for now it was almost eerily silent except for the buzzing in my head.

"Did you live in California?" I managed to ask.

"For about a year," she replied. I felt my conversational abilities returning and regurgitated another question.

"Anything about it you miss?"

She thought for a moment before saying, "Good weed and twenty four hour drive thru liquor stores."

"No shit?" I asked in near disbelief. I had grown up in the Bible belt. Liquor stores were only open from 2 to 9 pm and were never open on Sundays.

"No shit," she confirmed. "Speaking of weed. You wanna burn one?"

"Sure," I said. I slunk into one of the other chairs and made a feeble attempt at charm.

"I always thought it was weird that you could get a driver's license before you could buy alcohol. You'd think it be better if folks learned to hold their liquor first."

To my surprise she actually laughed. Not a gut buster by any means, but still a lovely little guffaw. She pulled a bag of some good looking chronic out of her pocket and some papers.   I tried to be the gentlemen.

"Since you're the philanthropist I'll twist it up if you want," I offered. She held the goods out to me. Our hands touched at the exchange, and I was so dorked out I actually felt a rush.

"Why thank you," she said.

"Don't mention it," I politely chimed. I set the weed in my lap and snagged a pinch from the bag. I was feeling pretty good, but when my hands went to work on the weed I was betrayed. They were too shaky. The weed broke up easily enough, and I was able to fill the paper, but my twisting abilities were too impaired. I ripped the paper, spilling some of the herb.

"Fuck," I said and tried to regroup. I got another paper and gathered what I could of the spill, then added a touch more to compensate for what was lost. I steadied my hands and went for the twist. I ripped the god damn joint again. The instantly exasperated look on my face made Vicki laugh, and I was thankfully able to take it all in stride.

"I guess you better roll this up," I admitted, scooping up the contents and handing the bag back to her.

"You okay?" she asked, her sly smile telling me she knew full well the cause of my dysfunction.

"Yeah, I'm fine. I'm just tweaking pretty good. That's some wicked shit," I said, referring to the high octane fuel that boiled my blood.

Vicki pulled a fresh paper and began filling it.

"I'm going to have to get more soon," she said. I wasn't sure if she meant the weed or the crank. I took a shot in the dark.

"Do you go all the way back to Cali to get it?" I casually inquired, figuring she wouldn't go that far for weed.

"Yep," she just as casually replied. I sat back and thought of what it would be like to see the ocean. I'd never been out of the state. Vicki finished her roll and licked the paper. Her dark eyes found mine, and I watched those twin pools swirl with their mysterious waters. What she said next almost knocked me out of my chair.

"You want to go with me?" she asked, and held out the finished joint. It was perfect. I tried to catch my breath and told myself I'd heard her correctly. I nervously sought verification.

"For real?" I practically whispered as I took the joint from her hand.

God damn her smile. She shed it once more, and I melted like microwaved butter.

"Sure. Why not?" she seemed to say as much to herself as to me. I didn't care either way. I damn well knew my answer.

"Hell yeah I wanna go. When we leaving?" I blurted like a kid who just got offered a trip to Disneyland.

"Let's leave tonight," she said as pretty as could be, with all the grace of someone who only knew how to live in the moment. While I hesitated, she produced a lighter and flicked it before me. I lit the joint and breathed deep.

"Tonight?" I asked and immediately kicked myself, fearing she'd reconsider, and the whole thing would never manifest. Her next statement washed those fears away.

"Sure, Let's just drive away right now and not tell anyone. That way no one will even know we're on a run."

I took another hit and passed the j. She had a good point. If word got around we were going to Cali to bring back more of the high grade danger dust I'd just sampled, it might bring too much attention. Somebody was always getting busted, and I certainly didn't want to be the next one to go down. As a lower level street junkie I had more or less remained a non entity on the cops' radar, but that would change fast if I started slinging the pure shit with this princess.

"Let's do it." I said. "We can take my car. I'll drive."

2

Desmond awoke with a chill in the dead before the dawn. The moon was now long gone, and a deep darkness engulfed him. He sat up and shivered, completely lost. He felt like he was almost floating outside of his body. His limbs were ghosts and his heartbeat seemed too distant. Panic tried to rise within him, and he forced himself to club it back, until it whimpered in a corner of his mind.

Slowly, he got to his feet and looked up at the starry sky. His eyes adjusted enough to dispel his irrational fears. He told himself there was no way he was going to die in one square mile of young forest. All he had to do was go a straight line in any direction and he'd hit a road. He didn't really want to try to navigate in the dark, but he was cold and movement would warm him up.

He decided to go for it. He reached into his pocket and pulled out his cigarette lighter. He walked slow and steady with one hand in front of him to divert sneaky tree limbs that eagerly awaited the chance to poke an eye out. His other hand flicked the lighter on and off like a lazy strobe light so it wouldn't get too hot. From a distance it must a have looked like a willow wisp   drifted through the trees.

Luck was with him. After only ten minutes he came to a fence. He held the lighter high and peered through the dark. He could see that there was a dirt road on the other side of it. Desmond tucked the lighter away and very carefully pushed down on the barbed wire and stooped through to the other side. His long hair briefly snagged some of the wire, but he tore it free, ignoring the pain. He was in no mood for that kind of bullshit right now.

He stumbled out of the ditch and got his lighter back out to take a closer look at the road. He had drifted mostly to his right while he walked, so instead of heading due south, he'd gone west and hit the next road over that way. He could tell by the ground before him where he more or less had wound up. It couldn't be the road that lay due west because that one was paved, and the road he'd left behind was pale gravel. The road now before him was good old Oklahoma red dirt.

He turned to his left and retired the lighter. He had just enough natural light to stay on the easy path before him. With no burden of movement his mercurial mind roamed with the residual effects of the previous evening's doings. Like myself, Desmond had a philosophical bend to his thinking, and he found himself dwelling on what the point of his existence was.

It would be something of an understatement to say that he didn't have a very positive outlook at the time. When he thought about life, he usually felt cheated. As far as he was concerned the American dream was a lie, and he was a prisoner in a world where the deck was stacked against him. The whole idea of earning a living was absurd to him. He was alive, what was there to earn? Left to their own devices people would feed and shelter themselves without coercion, and would help their loved ones do the same. He had absorbed enough wisdom from his elders on the reservation to understand that was all the work nature intended. Did it really take forty hours a week completing mostly arbitrary tasks for the next 40 years to constitute an acceptable contribution? Who did that serve and to what end?

To Desmond it was obvious that people in white society were the ultimate slaves. They thought they were free, so they worked hard to buy what was already theirs in order for other men to fancy themselves kings. The white man's dance was like a siren song. The moves were enchanting and the costumes dazzling, but it drained the life from everything within its circle of vanity.

These realizations were almost mundane to him. He had lived with them since birth, but they were shining revelations for me when he shared his thoughts. Many of his insights greatly influenced my own thinking during this tenuous time in my life, and for that I would always be grateful.

What any of these and other hypothesizes meant in the larger scheme of things remains a matter of speculation, but I can tell you this much. In questioning our world, we questioned ourselves and sought honest answers. We also shared both the questions and our answers freely. Sharing gave us the power to reach for something more, something that was more precious than gold yet completely immaterial. It helped us realize that we were more than the sum of our parts, even in spite of our many flaws, and when you know that, you know all that really matters.

3

I cruised down the I-40 westbound lane with my crystal princess by my side. At the moment life wasn't just good. It was fucking good.

"Ya know, I've never been out of the state before," I confided.

"Really?" she said, probably not all that surprised.

"Yep. Furthest I've been from Oklahoma City was when I was a kid. My mom and me went down to the Ozark Wilderness. I remember my parents saying we were just a few miles from the Arkansas line, and I was pretty little, so I got all excited like were travelling to another planet or something,"

I immediately felt embarrassed by this outpouring, so I quickly added, "It's dumb. I know."

"No," she assured. "It's not dumb at all. How old were you?"

"Six or seven."

She got a fun gleam in her eye.

"When we cross the state line, we should stop and have some kind of ceremony."

I laughed. That was a hoot. I thought she was pulling my leg.

"Really?' I asked.

"Absolutely," she confirmed with a straight face.

My mind tried to envision a ritual. I inadvertently pictured us standing on the side of the road dressed in robes, shooting meth into an armadillo while we sang the Star Spangled Banner. I laughed again.

"I can't imagine what to do," I lied.

She took my free hand and held it to her chest and spoke in a melodramatic falsetto.

"We'll kiss under the stars and say, 'Goodbye, Oklafuckinghoma!'"

I couldn't help but laugh a third time. I met her eyes and a kiss seemed inevitable. I leaned toward her, and she leaned into me. Then I swerved into those annoying bumps on the side of the road, and had to return my attention to the wheel.

"Shit," I cursed and got steady in my lane again. When we were cruising smooth again I looked over. She was staring at me with a sad smile, and I struggled to pay attention to the road. God, she was beautiful. There was an awkward silence. She took my right hand and held it while she impaled me with those depthless eyes. I thought for a moment I saw tears swimming in them. A more mysterious person I have yet to meet.

"You have a good heart," she said with the utmost sincerity. I was somewhat taken aback by the observation. If I had been asked to name one of my character traits that probably wouldn't have been a first guess. My surprise at her appraisal must have showed for she quickly apologized.

"Sorry, I know that kinda came out of nowhere. Didn't mean to put you on the spot."

I wasn't offended in the slightest and would have said as much, but I still pondered the accuracy of her statement about my heart.

"Sometimes I wonder,' I said. "I hope you're right."

She still had a hold of my hand, and she gave it a tender squeeze.

"I am," she assured. She leaned over and kissed my cheek. It was only a peck, but my already viciously cycling blood flowed to my head in a sudden torrent. She laid her head on my shoulder, and we drove on hand in hand.

CHAPTER 9

It's time yet again for another addendum to our story, for we are at the point where Barry and I parted ways. Permanently. Of course, I didn't know that at the time, but regardless, I would be negligent if I failed to at least provide some conjecture on the details of his journey as well as my own.

After I took off with Vicki, Barry tweaked his ass off playing chess with Bill. He'd lost every game and was about to lose the next one. It seemed like he'd been playing for hours, and with good cause, because it had indeed been hours. When you were high, time whizzed by faster than an astronaut parked on an event horizon, and after you returned to Earth, you found yourself amazed that hundreds of years had passed.

For Barry, the return trip was initiated by the need for a smoke and another blast. He stared dumbly at the board, not caring anymore about the outcome.

"Here, goddamnit. Bishop to Queen 3," he hastily decided. Bill's bushy eyebrows twitched behind his sunglasses. He reached over and moved a mere pawn.

"I believe that's checkmate," he consolingly informed Barry, who immediately stood at the declaration and reached for his cigs.

"This game's fucking retarded," he assured himself. He popped a smoke from the pack and resisted the urge to smack the smug look off of Bill's blind face. He lit his cigarette, forgetting that Bill didn't like folks to smoke indoors.

"Cigarettes outside please, Barry. Thank you," he said in a parental tone. Barry redoubled his efforts not to punch him and strode out the door.

He walked through the living room eyeing the tray on Bill's table. He resisted the impulse to steal some of the dope. He knew Bill could hear a cow piss a mile away so he tore his gaze from temptation and headed out onto the back porch.

Barry stood in the night air and puffed on his smoke. He noticed my car was gone.

"Fucker's out getting him some," was his immediate supposition as to my whereabouts.   He took a drag off his smoke and stepped off the porch for a stroll around the property. He took note of a small tool shed that looked long neglected and a lawn full of already overgrown grass. He then moseyed around the house to the front yard while debating his options. He didn't feel like walking home, and he didn't feel like hanging out with Bill anymore. If worse came to worse he'd just call home and tell Cass to pick him up in their mom's car. It wouldn't be the first time Barry had been such high maintenance. Cass knew that when the phone rang at odd hours it was surely Barry calling for a ride, and if he didn't pick up there'd be hell to pay.

Barry decided to see if the keys to the Camaro might be dangling in the ignition. He had no qualms about borrowing it for a few quick errands. He walked over and stuck his hand in the open window. He felt the empty slot.

"Shit. Plan B," he muttered. It looked like Cass would be getting that call after all. It was less than ideal, but he could at least get a ride to Aaron's before the sun came up and his mom got up for work. She was the one person on this earth who could still put the fear of God in him, so the last thing he wanted was for her to wake up for work and find her car missing. She was a hard woman, and Barry knew he was broken from her mould. He'd never raised a hand to her, and he never would.

His father was a different story. The beating's Barry had taken when he was younger had been repaid in kind over the last couple years, until their relationship evolved into a shared disregard. On the rare occasions when they were both even home at the same time, they had no words or acknowledgment between them. Barry sometimes said that the only pearl of wisdom his father had ever bestowed were the words, "You either take an ass whooping or you give you one."

Presently, Barry came back from his mental meanderings and reminded himself of a small to do before he borrowed Bill's phone.

"I need to get Blindman to front me some of that pure."

Motivated by this thought, he stomped his smoke and headed back inside.

Barry entered Bill's living room and found him sitting in his chair, rigging up a shot. He figured it was as good of a time as any to ask him for a loan.

"I don't suppose you'd be willing to front me a teener?" he asked point blank. He wasn't one for subtlety, but the question didn't exactly catch Bill by surprise.

"I think I can manage that," he answered, his hands never veering from their current mission."I'll need you to bring me back a little more than the usual market value though," he added.

"How much more?" Barry asked. He'd expected an increase in the going rate.

"Two hundred," replied Bill matter of factly. Barry whistled.

"That's almost as much as an eight ball," he objected, only to see if Bill would waver.

He did not. He just went about his business as if he hadn't heard a thing.

Barry saw negotiation wasn't an option, so he added, "But considering the quality I think that'll be just fine." He already had a plan. He still had the crank he'd got from Hollister. He'd sell the part he'd cut, and then he'd cut the rest and sell that too. That would be enough to pay back both Hollister and Bill, and he'd be able to save all the good stuff for himself.

Barry congratulated himself on his business skills and waited for Bill to confirm the deal. The sightless fellow's hands were almost finished with their work. He had the shot rigged up and he held the syringe up to tap out the air bubbles. He primed the point by using the tip of his index finger to tell when it was ready. Satisfied with that, he put the cap back on and set the rig down on the tray.

"Alright then. I should weigh that out for you before I do this," he said and lovingly patted his waiting shot of dope. He opened a drawer on the table next to him and pulled out some baggies. Barry made small talk.

"Looks like Todd and your girl opted for some private time. His car's gone and there's a gray Camaro sitting out front."

"That would be Vicki's, although I can't attest to the color," joked Bill. He dropped some rocks into a baggie and felt it for accuracy with his sensitive fingers. I'd once tested his ability to measure dope in this way and found to my astonishment that he was as accurate as any scale.

Barry knew of Bill's skills as well, so instead of scrutinizing the measurement, his thoughts lingered on my whereabouts.

"I bet that fucker is out getting him some. Lucky bastard. She's probably got some good pussy," he said enviously. Bill paused and looked as directly at Barry as he could manage.

"She's almost like a daughter to me, so please keep your speculations to yourself," he chided. Barry wasn't shamed in the least.

"Well I hate to break it to you, Dad," he sarcastically retorted, "but your girl is a hot little potato, and if I know Todd he'll be banging that shit real soon, if he isn't already."

Bill set the baggie down, visibly perturbed, but not for the exact reasons one might think.

"I seriously doubt that Vicki would let herself be seduced," he said.

Barry jumped to the first conclusion his misogynist brain came to.

"What's up? She a dike or something?" he tactfully inquired. There was a window of silence where Bill pondered how much to divulge to Barry. He decided it was okay to just tell him the truth.

"No," he said sadly. "Vicki has AIDS."

Barry was at once stunned and repulsed by the revelation.

"No fucking shit?" he gasped. "You sure she doesn't still fuck around?"

"She wouldn't do anything harmful to Todd. She's very open about it. He probably already knows," Bill assured and went back to filling the baggie so he could send his now unwanted guest on his way. Fortunately for Bill, Barry was still feeling restless, even more so now that he'd received such uncomfortable news. He reminded himself to call Cass.

"Regardless of whatever they're up to, I'm out of a ride," he said. "You still got a phone?"

Bill nodded and gestured toward an adjacent room.

"In the kitchen on the wall."

Barry hopped to his feet and marched out. He passed through the open doorway and into the small kitchen. He saw the phone in its described location and snatched it from its cradle. Then he dialed home and leaned against the wall while he waited for Cass to pick up. Sometimes it took a few rings for him to wake up, particularly if he'd gotten shitfaced the night before. As for the chance of their mom or dad waking up at the incessant sound, they'd just yell at Cass to get his ass up and answer it. That kid didn't get very many breaks.

Finally, he picked up. Barry spoke before Cass could get a word out.

"Come get me. I'm at Blindman's place."

There was no reply. Barry was instantly annoyed.

"Hello?" he said a couple more times, and then listened closely. He could just hear the sound of Cass' quick breaths.

"What the fuck are you doing, dumbass? I can hear you breathing. Get the goddamn car and get over here."

Cass finally found his tongue and his soft, nervous voice replied, "Kirby's dead, Barry."

Time slammed on the brakes, and Barry flew through the windshield. He found himself in a sudden stupor, trying to digest his brother's words.

"What the fuck did you just say?" he spluttered.

Cass elaborated in a forced whisper.

"Kirby's fuckin' dead. The cops were here. You killed him when you rammed his head into that pole."

Barry hit free fall. He barely heard Cass' next few words.

"Barry?" he asked, then quickly added, "Don't come home, they're watching the house," pause, "you still there?" another pause, "…Barry?"

Cass would get no answer except for the terrible sound of his brother repeatedly slamming the phone against the cradle on Bill's kitchen wall.

2

"So. Do you feel any different?" Vicki asked. We'd just crossed the state line into the Texas panhandle. We were still holding hands, which was all the ceremony I needed.

"I do," I honestly replied. "I feel like the road has no end."

All of a sudden she didn't seem to share my optimism.

"All roads end somewhere," she said sadly. I was still in the dark about her illness, so at the time I just took her statement at face philosophical value.

"Maybe that's just a matter of perspective," I waxed. "Roads aren't really straight lines at all. They're an infinite web of possibilities."

I turned to her, pleased with my wit to see if she would posit a counter theory. She did not, but only stared at me with her Mona Lisa smile. This time I caught a sense of something dark within her.

"You had some bad shit happen to you out west, huh?" I assumed.

"I've had bad shit happen to me everywhere. It's not so exclusive," she rejoined. Her hand left mine. We both went quiet for a moment at that. Speaking for myself, I can't say the silence was exactly uncomfortable. I wasn't used to feeling this strongly about anyone, so even this bitter moment had its sweetness. I had my own heartbreak stories, and was in no way surprised by the fact that she had hers. Still, I wanted to lighten the mood, so I made another lame attempt at humor.

"There is no gravity. The earth just sucks."

She didn't laugh, but the quip earned a smile and seemed to shift the energy.

"Did you just make that up?' she asked.

"Nah, I don't remember where I got it from. It's just stuck with me," I humbly replied.

That sad distant look came back to her eyes.

"Funny how things can work like that," she said. I fixed my eyes on her. Damn, she was a spooky one. I couldn't figure her out at all, and that only made her all the more attractive. She met my puppy dog gaze, and her eyes teared up.

"I need to tell you something," she almost whispered. My heart picked up a few beats.

"What?"

She hesitated. Only in retrospect would I realize it was then that she almost told me she had AIDS, but she faltered at the last moment, choosing a different truth instead.

"You make me feel really good," she said.

I didn't know what to say. I'd never loved so one so much, so fast, in all of my life. I retook her hand in mine.

"I'm feeling pretty good too," I managed, trying to maintain eye contact without driving off the road. Her free hand reached up and caressed my face. She leaned over and kissed me again. This time it was ever so softly on the lips. She then drew away, hand and all, to recline in her chair.

"I think I'm going to try to sleep for a little bit," she said. I was bummed that she had withdrawn from her closer proximity, but I wasn't about to pout at this stage of the game so I rolled with it.

"No worries. I'll probably keep driving for awhile. When I get tired I'll get us a hotel somewhere," I said as casual as I could.

She said no more, but closed her eyes as a glorious sun rose in my rearview mirror.

I drove on, feeling truly happy for the first time I could ever remember.

3

Barry pulsed like a reanimated corpse in Bill's chair. He'd just finished doing another shot. His eyes were glassy, and his face was a strange combination of vacant and twitchy.

The same sun that was creeping into my rearview now filtered through the windows of Bill's house. The light peeked over the sills and spilled onto the wall.

Barry watched it slowly crawl down the wall and over the floor, where it gradually illuminated Bill's dead body in a haunting glow. Blood surrounded his head in a macabre halo. His sunglasses lay at the edge of the crimson pool, next to the ruptured phone.

After Barry had finished whacking the phone against the wall in the kitchen, he ripped the cord out of the wall and used it on Bill with the same heedless fury. The coroner's report would describe the cause of death as 'blunt force trauma', which seemed to me a bit of an understatement.

Barry tore his eyes away from Bill and rose to his feet. He looked down at the tray of beautiful pure crystal on the table and stood staring at it. He suddenly sprung like a bear trap and kicked the table over, tray and all. He then proceeded to destroy the interior of the house. Furniture was flipped over, shelves were emptied, and anything breakable was broken. When he kicked over the lamp table between the two chairs, the drawer popped out, and Bill's gun skittered across the floor. It was an old Browning 9mm from his days in the Army. Barry picked it up and checked the clip. Fully loaded. He tucked it behind him and made his way through the kitchen, where he spilled a rack of dishes over and kicked in some cabinets.

Finally, he exited to the back porch and lit a cigarette with an eerily steady hand that contrasted his sweaty, wild face.

His eyes darted around the yard and fell on the small tool shed. He took a deep drag and made his way across the yard. The shed was padlocked so Barry pulled the gun, cocked the hammer, and blew the lock off. The door creaked open, and he peered in at the neatly organized assortment of tools. Before Bill had lost his sight he worked in the construction biz, and though he rarely used his old tools anymore he still kept his things tidy. He would spend hours arranging and cleaning them as he reminisced on better days.

Barry stepped inside and tugged a cord that hung from an overhead light. It flickered on, and he stood there with the gun dangling by his side, taking hard pulls off of his smoke. He absently set the gun on a work table and tried to decide if there was anything of use to him in here. He briefly considered taking a chainsaw, but then passed it up as too impractical. He was about to exit when he noticed a flat wooden box on the floor under a low shelf. He stepped closer and knelt down to lift the lid.

What he saw inside made him crack a smile that would chill a hyena's blood.

"Oh hell yes," he whispered in near ecstasy.

Barry replaced the lid and dragged the box out. It was heavy, but the artificial strength in his veins was more than sufficient to enable him to do the job.

4

Desmond trudged up the driveway to where Gerald's trailer house sat behind a small row of elm trees. He was relieved to see his mom's car was gone. He was in no hurry to explain where he'd been or what he'd been up to. The morning sun seemed to rise slowly in the sky, reluctant to take on its daily burden.

When Desmond came around the edge of the trees, he saw a deer standing in the yard eating the dewy grass. He stopped, and the deer raised its head. They both stood there regarding each other. The deer was poised to spring away at a moment's notice, but Desmond made no aggressive movements. He stood calmly, mesmerized by the statuesque creature.

A low distant boom, like a megaton firecracker, broke the silence. The deer's ears pivoted toward the sound, but its eyes never left Desmond. Slowly, it lowered its head and took a tentative bite of grass.

Desmond thought about the first time he had ever seen a deer. It had been when he was little and still lived on the reservation. He'd been sitting at his kitchen table with his Uncle Billy, who was the hardest drinking, hell raising, self proclaimed wagon burner he'd ever known. A deer had trotted past their window and paused under a nearby tree. Desmond had sat there staring at the animal in much the same way he was now. Billy noticed his captivation, and quietly asked him a seemingly simple question.

"What do you see out there?" he casually queried as he took a bite of oatmeal. Desmond cocked his head at the question. He wasn't sure what Billy was getting at.

"Um. A deer," he hesitantly replied. "What do you see?"

Billy swallowed his oatmeal and took a sip of his coffee. He set down the cup and eyed Desmond with the beautiful severity many of his people possessed.

"I see myself," he said with no hint of humor or sarcasm.

Desmond didn't really get it at the time, but now he had a better sense of what his uncle had perhaps meant. At the very least he certainly felt a sense of empathy with the creature before him. He took a slow step forward, quietly hoping it would let him draw nearer. It did not, but instead did what deer do and suddenly bounded away. He watched it elegantly glide through a thicket of trees and leap over a fence overgrown with bramble.

Desmond felt a sense of envy at its fluid grace, its sheer ability to slip so smoothly out of any situation it felt uncomfortable in.

He took a deep sigh and walked up to the door to his house. He opened it up and stepped inside to find the place exactly as it had been left days before. Shelves were naked where Sylvia's knick knacks had been shattered in Gerald's fury, and ceramic shards littered the carpet. An end table lay on its side and everything seemed to be in disarray. The blood stain on the floor had congealed into a nasty black spot where a few glutted houseflies buzzed lazily about.

Desmond left the door open to clear the musty air and went to the kitchen to get some food. He was mentally and physically exhausted, and he hadn't eaten in three days. Both his belly and his soul longed to be filled. While he often doubted whether he'd ever sate the one, for now he could at least take care of the other.

5

Barry approached the Camaro with hammer in hand. He didn't exactly know how to hotwire a car, but he had a technique that worked just as well.

He opened the driver's door and pulled a long flathead screwdriver out of his back pocket. He bent over and placed the head of the screwdriver in a seam on the steering column and whacked the end of it with the hammer. It took four tries, but then the column cracked open like an egg. Next, he jammed the screwdriver into the crack and pried it up enough to get the hammer's claws under the seam. He pulled back, snapping a section of plastic off to reveal the ignition rod. The hammer and screwdriver were tossed aside. Barry reached into his other back pocket and produced a pair of vice grips. He adjusted the width, then clamped them down on the rod and pulled back. The Camaro coughed to life. He sat down and closed the door.

The car sputtered and died. Barry reached up to pull the rod again when he heard the same low distant boom

Desmond and the deer experienced. Barry thought maybe it was a shotgun blast somewhere the next mile over to the south, but the depth of the sound made him second guess that theory. At any rate, he didn't linger on it much. He had his own crazy agenda. He pulled the rod, and the Camaro fired up again. He revved the engine and put it in gear. He then drove around the house to the shed where his new toys waited.

He parked the car and hopped out. He entered the shed and first grabbed the gun off the work table and tucked it away. Next, he reached down and dragged the heavy box over to the Camaro. He opened the passenger door then bent down to lift the box. He spread his legs, took a deep breath, and hauled it up with all the strength his stout frame could muster. He got it into the air and tried to set it gently on the seat, but it slipped and banged down onto the running board. The lid popped off, and Barry's heart almost stopped in expectation of immediate disaster.

Inside was an almost full case of construction grade TNT, a leftover from before Bill's accident.

"Not yet," Barry cooed to himself. "Not yet."

He steadied himself and lifted again, getting the box up onto the seat. He slid it into place then picked up the lid. Before he placed it over his haul, he stood admiring the neat rows of sticks and told himself if he was gonna go out, then he was going out with one hell of a bang.

Barry had never run from anything in his life, and he wasn't about to start now. Even the drugs were never an escape for him. It was just the only business opportunity in town worth pursuing. With his sad prospects of neighborhood domination threatened, he was determined to leave a mark no one would soon forget.

And he would do it in spades.

CHAPTER 10

I awoke on the bed in a hotel room in Tucumcari, New Mexico. I'd driven until my vision started to double before I hopped off the Interstate at the first viable exit I came to. After paying for the room, I lifted Vicki's still sleeping body out of my car and carried her inside to lay her on the bed. She stirred only long enough to ask me to lie beside her. I closed and locked the door, then gladly obliged. We slept most of the day away, and I personally would have slept longer if not for the sound of Vicki sitting at the table rigging up a shot.

I opened first one eye and then the other. Her hands were shaking with anticipation for her fix. She hastily drew water from a paper cup and doused a spoon full of crystal. She flipped the syringe around and mixed the water and rock until they combined into that viscous volatile state we both loved and knew so well. Completing that, she plopped a cotton ball into its center and lowered the needle. In her fervor I could see that she had the bevel on the needle turned the wrong way, so I spoke up.

"Bevel down," I muttered sleepily. She jumped at the sound of my voice.

"What?" she asked, annoyed by the interruption.

I ignored the small, unnecessary sting in my heart. Impatience when you were jonesing for your fix was a crime everyone was guilty of, and it didn't matter if it was meth or cocaine, cigarettes or caffeine, television or collecting exotic pets.

"You're going to barb the needle," I rephrased. She looked at her positioning and adjusted.

"Shit," she said. "Thanks. I get a little shaky when I wake up."

"No worries," I replied. "What time is it?"

"I don't know. Evening, I suppose."

She was none too concerned about the time. She pulled back the plunger and sucked up the thick amber fluid. I sat up and stretched.

"I can't believe I actually fell asleep," I remarked.

Vicki finished drawing her shot and stood up.

"When your body really needs the rest, it takes it," she said as she walked towards the john. "There's more on the table if you want some. I'm going to do this in bathroom. I don't like to do it in front of anyone. I shake too much."

"Um. Ok," I said, a little amused by her shyness. I wondered how long she'd been living this lifestyle. I figured it was either much shorter or much longer than my own excursion. Like me, she wore a long sleeved shirt, so I couldn't really tell how chewed up her arms were.

She paused at the bathroom door.

"Pretty glamorous, huh?" she said.

"Is what it is," I consoled, not the least bit put off by her need for privacy. She gave me a warm smile and disappeared into the bathroom, closing the door behind her.

I hopped up and went to the table, suddenly eager for my own shot. I sat down and wet a finger, then stuck it inside the bag of dope she'd left and removed it for a quick taste.

"Breakfast of champions," I said, despite the fact that it was well past noon. I reached for my flannel shirt, and fished out a syringe I had stashed inside a seam. I set it on the table and saw the TV remote sitting nearby, so I grabbed it and turned on the tube for some background noise while I prepared my morning feast. A news reporter popped up on the screen. I looked to my labors, and at first only vaguely heard what the talking head on the screen was saying, but as its discourse soaked in, my attention was grasped.

"As you can see, there are police and fire crews on the ground. No survivors have yet been found. Medical personnel are there as well, helping to sift through the rubble. Traffic here in Oklahoma City has been completely closed to the downtown area."

I looked up and saw a big office building that had been blown to shit. It looked like a scene from a science fiction movie. I now watched closely and listened intently to what the reporter said.

"Just a horrible tragedy here in America's heartland. FBI officials are gathering what information they can. Several terrorist organizations have already taken credit for the blast, which is often the case. However, officials are not able to confirm anything at this time, except that the explosion was certainly not accidental."

What I was seeing was the remains of the Alfred P. Murrah Federal Building. It was April 19, 1995, the day of the Oklahoma City bombing. This was the source of the distant, intense boom that both Desmond and Barry had heard earlier that same day. Considering my outlaw self image, I wouldn't be as shocked as others to later learn the atrocious act was committed by one of our own veterans. However, like many of my contemporaries in this reddest of states, at the time I made immediate assumptions about who could be responsible.

"Hey, Vicki," I hollered. "Some crazy ass'd sand niggers bombed Oklahoma City."

No reply came. I muted the TV and walked over to the bathroom.

"Did you hear?" I asked and placed my hand against the door. It wasn't shut all the way, and so it eased open.

The image I saw before me will stay emblazoned on my brain till the day I die.

Vickie was topless. She had her back to me, but she stood in front of the mirror, so I could see her front as well as her back. Her body was covered in numerous small dark sores. She had the needle buried in her left nipple, her face rigid with concentration. I stared dumbly as she registered the shot. Blood flooded the chamber, and she drove it home.

She looked at me in the mirror as her eyes glazed over, and her sad smile spoke volumes I didn't care to comprehend. I quickly closed the door, and stammered in my speech.

"I'm sorry. I forgot you don't like to be watched. I didn't mean to see you. Fuck. Fuck, I did not want to see that."

I walked back to the table, needing my own fix more than ever. I turned off the TV, forgetting all about the drama in my homeland. I went back to prepping my breakfast and tried to process what the sores on Vicki's body meant.

I was flexing my arm, trying to get a vein to rise when Vicki came out of the bathroom. I paused.

"Sorry again for busting in like that," I said.

"I'm sorry too," she returned and walked to the table. She sat down opposite me, her face melancholy yet flushed with fresh adrenaline. I spoke next.

"I didn't know you'd be in there…" I paused, at a sudden loss for words. "…like that."

Her melancholy look took on a air of resolve.

"Don't worry about it. What's done is done."

I sat in stasis with my unspent needle dangling in my hand. I wanted to ask her about the sores. I didn't have to. She brought it up first.

"Do you know what the sores on my body are from?"

I didn't at the moment, so I offered my best guess.

"From this," I said, holding up my shot. She shook her head.

"No. At least not directly."

"What then?" I asked, suddenly realizing they might be from some disease. My heart shuddered at the thought, but what she said next made it sink like a lead weight.

"They're from AIDS," she said, her face a mask of regret and pain.

I went blank. All of the color drained out of me, turning me into a pale piece of rotten meat.

"Oh," I said, more deadpan than a monotone mortician. She sounded equally drained.

"I was going to tell you."

"When?" I heard myself say, not really caring what the answer was.

"I don't know. Soon."

I didn't believe her. The first stirrings of anger swirled at the bottom of an internal chasm. I resumed flexing my arm and got the needle in place.

"We can still be friends, Todd. That's all I ever wanted and still want. A friend. Someone to hold me."

I barely heard her, but replied anyway.

"Sure. Friends till the end," I said, and the needle slid into my flesh. I registered and hit the plunger. The welcome rush washed over my disturbed mind. I tossed the needle on the table and sat there in a daze, ignoring her pleading eyes. When she reached out for my hand, I jerked it back like it'd been approached by a snake. I ignored the tears that welled in her eyes, and stared at the wall, lost in my own misery. All of my hopes and dreams for our trip together had disappeared as quickly as the bad medicine I had just pumped into my vein.

I felt only relief when she got up, opened the door, and stepped outside. If you think me callous, then you should know now that this was nothing compared to what was to come. I hope you can forgive me, for as I touched on in brief earlier in our story, I and most of my peers did not have an informed predisposition regarding AIDS. Ignorance and fear were the norm, and at the time I was no exception. Plus, the fact that I had fallen so quickly and deeply in love with her made my malaise all the more extreme.

The measure of the pendulum's swing to the left would be the measure of the swing to the right.

2

Desmond laid on his couch in an uneasy sleep. He dreamed about a time when he was ten and had been sent to the principal's office, which to my understanding was a common occurrence for him back then. According to Sylvia, he was quite the little hell raiser until he hit puberty, and then all that outward energy somehow moved inward, creating the bookish introvert I'd met and befriended.

In his dream, he was reliving another pivotal moment in his youth. He had gotten in trouble for disobeying his teacher and then yelling at her. He was pleading his case to the principal, who looked across a huge desk at him with a steady, unflinching gaze. Desmond cried, he was afraid he was going to get swats. He hated getting swats more than anything, not for the pain but because of the shame it brought. In desperation he told the principal the reason he was in trouble so often was because his mamma drank.

What the principal said in response would stick with him throughout his life, and he often reminded himself of the man's words.

"Desmond," he said. "That is called a crutch."

Apparently the look on Desmond's face said he didn't understand what the hell the man was talking about, so he elaborated.

"The crutch I'm talking about is in your mind. It's something you use to prop yourself up with not because you have to, but because you don't want to see the truth. And the truth here is that you won't benefit from blaming your mother."

Desmond still had nothing to say. The tears had stopped, and he just sat there looking up at him with a confused look on his face. The principal decided to break it down simple.

"The bottom line is that you are ultimately responsible for your own behavior. "

The words echoed and faded in his dream. The principal's big bald head dissolved with all other images at the sound of the front door opening. Desmond's alpha waves slowed to a crawl and cognition reached for the ignition.

He opened his eyes and saw his mother standing in the doorway. As she walked towards him, he wondered if he was still dreaming.

Sylvia walked across the small living room and sat beside him. She reached out and tucked his hair behind his ear and caressed his cheek. Desmond realized this indeed was not another dream, and slowly sat up, trying not look at the yellowing bruises on her face. He sat there in silence and let her lightly caress his face. Her eyes were swimming with emotion. He could smell alcohol on her, but that was to be expected under the circumstances.

"I can't stay here," she said. "I'm gonna be at Gladys' for a while."

Gladys was her sister. She lived about twelve miles away in the town of Crescent. She was a foul mouthed, headstrong woman who had an opinion on just about everything. Desmond liked her immensely, at least as long as he wasn't on her shit list for anything.

"They released Cole yesterday. Needless to say, he'll be staying with his daddy for a while. I don't know when we'll see him again. At the courthouse I reckon."

Desmond finally met his mom's intense, sad face. He looked around at the mess and realized he'd done nothing since he'd gotten home except eat and sleep.

"I'm sorry I didn't clean up, I was – "

Sylvia put a gentle hand to his mouth to hush him.

"We'll do it together," she said. He nodded, and swallowed the lump that rose in the back of his throat. It worked for a second, but then Sylvia broke down in tears, causing his internal dam to bust as well.

"I'm sorry, son. I'm so sorry," she cried. He held her in his arms.

"It's not your fault, mom," he assured. "It's not your fault."

They sat there on the couch and let the cleansing tears flow.

When the tide finally rolled back out they quietly went about the work of cleaning the place up. I can't even fathom the depth of what each of them felt. The reconciliation of the mother-son relationship is something I've never achieved in my own life, and I regret that I am unable to convey a sense of what this watershed moment meant for my friend. Even Desmond himself was either unable or unwilling to talk much about it. I think at the very least his trials made him ready to put aside his childish fears and be a man, whatever that means.

And this tender moment is where we'll leave Desmond be. There's not much more about his journey that I could effectively relay anyhow. What I can tell you is that he and his family soon moved away. Sylvia sold the land after a brief fight over it with Gerald's brother. Gerald left no will, but she was his legal spouse, so in the end she still got her due despite the extra hassle. When she got the money, her and Desmond moved to another town on the other side of the state.

To Desmond's credit he never did meth again. His experience over the last few days was sufficient to deter him from any more forays into society's underbelly. I'd like to tell you he even worked his way up to some grand life, but the truth is that he only did what most of us do. He worked a thankless job for less than he was worth, had babies, and paid taxes. Eventually, we would grow apart like many friends do.

We still talk from time to time, but it was our youthful angst that provided most of the collagen for our friendship, so as it fades away we talk less and less. Such is the way of things. It seems to me that people often use each other like newspapers, and once we're done reading what interests us, we toss each other aside. The friendships that last are the ones that always have something new to be written. I guess ours said what it had to say, or at least mine did because I'm the one who has changed the least. One of us decided to grow up, and the other decided to stay in Never Never Land.

3

Vicki and I once more cruised on our westward journey. The mood was considerably different from how it began. We'd barely exchanged a word between us after leaving the hotel. My drugged brain had crawled inside a shell and every time Vicki tried to ask me a question or break the ice in some way I either ignored her or gave one word answers, like those old standbys "sure" and "fine".

I vaguely took notice of her increased frustration. Both of us were amped, and I for one didn't really even know why I was still going anywhere with her. In a strange way we were both trying not to feel trapped by the other person.

"Are you going to say anything or are we gong to drive the rest of the way to California in silence?" she asked point blank.

"We need to stop for gas soon," I coolly replied, struggling to keep the lid on my emotions, which had turned into a giant pressure cooker. She must have been in a similar boat, because her face flushed redder than it already was.

"Maybe you should just drop me off in the next town, and I'll catch a bus," she said curtly.

Something inside me snapped. I slammed on the brakes.

A minivan swerved around us and blared its horn. I turned the wheel, and we skidded to a stop on the shoulder. More cars honked in disdain as they flew by us.

Vicki yelled in my face.

"What the hell is wrong with you!"

As dramatic as the skid had been, I felt strangely calmed by it, so I again replied with my cool tone.

"You're going to die."

She sat back, flabbergasted. "We're all going to die," she reasoned. I had no use for her logic, and I wasn't looking for a philosophical exchange so I put it to her bluntly.

"I don't want anything to do with you, and I don't want to love you," I said.

My use of the 'L' word caught her off guard, and she went on a rant.

"This isn't about love…this isn't about love. People like you don't how to love. You just know about running away. That's why you tweak out. You're running away from everything, and the only reason you thought you even cared about me was because I was helping you do it. What the fuck do you know about me or the world outside of your pathetic little neighborhood?"

She took a breath, and let that last line soak in. I didn't care for her observations, and I'd had enough of this road trip.

"Just get out. Get out of my fucking car," I told her.

"What? We're in the middle of nowhere," she spat as if I gave a shit.

"It's an interstate, someone will pick you up."

Our eyes locked, and I hated myself for the stirring of sympathy in my heart. She must have seen it as well because she wasn't ready to accept my demand.

"I don't believe you.'

I looked away. I couldn't meet those beautiful dark eyes. I was still drawn to her, but now the feeling was as repulsing as it was inviting. Her next words almost broke through my doubt and fear. They were delivered with softness and not the spite she'd just served.

"I know you felt something special for me and that now you're hurting. I felt it for you too. I was scared and couldn't bring myself to tell you the truth. I'm sorry. Can we just stop this and treat each other right?"

What I did next was the shittiest thing I've ever done in my life. I reached under my seat and got my gun. Looking back, I'm not sure exactly why I even did it. I only remember feeling an overwhelming emptiness wash over me. I figure the best explanation for my actions might be that even though her words rang true enough, I was not trying to open my heart. I was trying to bury it.

I pointed the gun at her face.

"Get the fuck out of my god damn car," I croaked as steadily as I could manage. She said nothing, but only sat there staring at me in pain and disbelief. I again felt sympathy scratching at its coffin lid. I was too weak to let it free.

"Get. Out."

Silent tears streamed down her face. She grabbed her bag, opened the door, and stumbled out of the car. She then slammed the door and started walking down the shoulder of I-40.

I lowered the gun and watched her go. I briefly contemplated putting the gun to my head and blowing my brains out. Instead I put the gun under the ashtray in its usual hiding place. I made myself feel like less of a dickhead by remembering I'd never even flipped off the safety. I pulled back onto the road, and when I passed her by I refused to look over.

That peculiar blankness once more fell over me for about a mile. Then I completely lost it. I was like the dishes on top of a table cloth that had been yanked out by a clumsy magician and thus fell, shattering on the floor.

I began banging my fist against the dash, and I screamed at the top of my lungs for her to be damned by God.

4

Hollister pulled into his long driveway and drove past the collection of junk he'd hoarded over the years. When he got near his double wide he saw a grey Camaro parked with the hood up and what looked like a box placed on top of the motor. He pulled up to it and stopped.

"What the hell?" he mumbled to himself. He didn't recognize the car and looked around to see if anyone was hanging out. No one was in sight so he put his truck in park and killed the engine. He heard another engine running, and it took him a moment to realize that it was the Camaro.

He reached in the glove box and grabbed his .357. He didn't know what was up with this car or where the owner was, and he wasn't taking any chances. He tucked the gun behind him and opened his door.

Hollister got out and stepped towards the Camaro with his eyes peeled. He got to the front of the car and took a closer look at the box. It looked to be made of metal or aluminum and was painted black. It was three feet long and only about six inches deep, and was set on the motor at a cockeyed angle, facing the warm noon sun.

Hollister leaned over and lifted the lid on the box to see rows of dynamite sweating from the heat. He quickly set the lid back down.

"God damn son of bitch!" he proclaimed and back pedaled away from the car. Then he heard a voice behind him.

"They starting to sweat yet?"

Hollister spun around to see Barry leaning against his truck. He had Bill's gun in his hand. Holly had heard the news about Kirby's demise, and the look on Barry's face was not a kind omen.

"I've heard that when dynamite gets hot it gets unstable and sweats pure nitroglycerin," said Barry in a conversational tone. Hollister didn't find himself in the mood for small talk.

"You're off the god damn deep end," he said, stating the obvious. Barry wasn't a bit offended by the observation.

"No," he said matter of fact. "I ain't."

Barry walked toward the Camaro. Holly circled out of the way and waited for an opportunity to draw his gun. Barry turned his back to him and peeked inside the box of explosives.

"Oh yeah," he cooed. "those are looking just about ready. Let's try one out."

Barry reached into the box to grab a stick. Hollister reached around his back for his gun.

"I ain't here to kill you, Holly," Barry said, making Hollister freeze. "Besides, you going to shoot at me while I'm standing in front of a box of dynamite?"

Hollister couldn't well argue with that logic, and silently cursed himself for being stupid enough to almost draw his pistol. He returned his hand to the front of his person and reluctantly decided to play this out.

Barry turned around with his Cheshire grin stretched across his manic face, holding a stick of sweaty dynamite.

"Ain't that pretty?" admired Barry. Hollister wasn't nearly as captivated.

"What the hell are you doing, Barry?" he asked. Barry didn't answer, but instead reared back, preparing to throw the stick into the air.

"Heads up," he cautioned, then lobbed the explosive through the sky in a high arc.

"God damn!" cursed Hollister and hit the dirt. Barry stood unflinching and watched the stick land twenty feet away near an old livestock feeder still partially filled water from the last rain.

The stick exploded on impact, launching water, dirt, and shrapnel towards the firmament. A jagged piece of metal landed close to Hollister as the debris fell back to earth.

"God damn insane motherfucker!" yelled Hollister. He knew he was in a bad spot. He was tempted to try and shoot Barry regardless of his proximity to the box. Fortunately, Barry's next statement offered a bit of relief.

"Well that settles it. The rumors are true. We should probably turn the motor off now though, huh?" he reasoned, or at least seemed to. He smiled at Hollister and saluted him with the gun he still held. He then moseyed around the car and reached in the window of the car to turn it off. The engine died and everything got real quiet. Barry strolled back around the car and leaned against the front end.

"So what do you think, Holly?" he asked as if it was a lazy Saturday, and they had nothing to do.

"I think I should have shot you while I had the chance. I'd a been doing you a favor."

Barry grinned big at that. He put the gun to his head. He cocked the hammer and his smile faded.

"Maybe I'll just do myself a favor."

Hollister had no objections.

"Go for it. Crazy bastard."

Barry glared at Hollister and spoke slowly, tasting each word.

"I ain't crazy. I just got no love for life anymore. So I don't fear death. Not mine or anyone else's."

Barry suddenly pointed the gun at Hollister. He fired. The bullet tore through Hollister's leg. He cried out in shock and pain as he fell to the ground. He reached for his gun, but Barry was already there to deliver a swift kick right in his face.

Hollister's gun fell to the ground, and Barry reached down to pick it up.

"Hell, this one's nicer than mine," he said. "Reckon I'll keep it."

He loomed over Hollister, training his own .357 on his torso. Holly pleaded.

"You said you weren't gonna kill me."

Barry shrugged. "I changed my mind."

He shot Hollister again, this time in the gut. Hollister screamed bloody murder and tried to buy his life back.

"I know where a shitload of crank is stashed. Couple pounds or more," he gasped.

Barry put the gun to his head.

"I've had enough," he said, and pulled the trigger. Hollister's brains decorated the dirt. Barry appraised his handiwork and made another observation.

"Now you have too."

5

Vicki walked down the shoulder of the interstate. Cars and 18 wheelers blew by her, whipping her hair into the air and flapping her loose clothes. She was in a dark spiral of depression. She blamed herself for what had happened and was seriously thinking about throwing herself in front of a big truck.

Perhaps the only thing that stopped her was the kindness of a total stranger. She saw a car brake as it passed her and pulled over to the side in what every hitchhiker knew was a sure sign of their next ride. Forgetting her suicidal urges, Vicki jogged toward the car. It took less than five minutes for her to get picked up.

The car, a four door Lincoln, waited patiently for her to approach the passenger side. The window rolled down and Vicki trained her eyes on a kindly looking old man dressed in his Sunday best. He was in fact coming from his niece's wedding in the next town over.

"You need a ride, young lady?" he asked. Vicki looked him over. He exuded safe so she nodded and opened the door. She sat down, and he introduced himself.

"Howdy, name's Ned Patton."

He didn't offer his hand but looked at her expectantly. She gave only a brief intro.

"Vicki."

He nodded and put the car in gear. He'd actually picked up many hitchhikers over the years and never passed anyone by if he could help it. He figured that all who wander are not lost, and it was his Christian duty to help the unfortunate traveler whenever possible. If a contemporary displayed shock at his liberality he always said he'd never had a negative experience from any of the folks he picked up. He for sure met some strange characters here and there, but as far as he was concerned it took all kinds to make the world go round. The Lord was the only one who needed to know what it all meant, and Ned was quite satisfied to leave it at that. His only duty was to be kind and honest.

"So, where you headed?' he asked as he pulled back onto the road. Vicki sunk into her seat, looking both morose and windswept.

"I don't know."

Ned raised an eyebrow at that.

"You don't know?"

Vicki stared out the window, not caring to meet his questioning gaze.

"I don't know," she reiterated. "So if you could just keep speeding me along, I'm sure I'll get there in record time."

He didn't really know what to say to that. Her gravity was immense. So much that it actually reminded him of a soldier he'd met in the war after he had to have both his legs amputated. That young man had said he felt endlessly hollow, completely empty inside. By the looks of the young woman sitting next to him now, he thought she must be feeling pretty much the same.

"You got kin around these parts?" he probed.

Vicki shook her head and continued staring out the window. After a lengthy pause, Ned went for another question.

"You need to call someone?"

At first he didn't think she was going to answer or say anything at all, but then she turned to him and spoke softly.

"There's no one to call. Just roads that lead and roads that end."

Ned nodded gravely. "I see," he said. "Well, I'm going as far as Santa Rosa. I can take you by the mission if you need a place to stay and figure things out. My sister works there, so I can assure you the folks are kind and the food is good."

Vicki couldn't help but smile at his simple courtesy.

"Is there a bus station?"

He nodded. "There is. It's a littl'un, but it's serviceable."

"That'll do," she replied.

Satisfied that he at least got a destination out of her, he was content to end his questions. If she wanted to say more he'd leave that up to her. He found that most times people would tell you more after a little quiet time than they would if you tried to pry answers out of them.

Vicki, however, would be an exception, and they drove the rest of the way in silence. For years afterward he would sometimes think of her and wonder if she ever found her way.

CHAPTER 11

Some of the following segments have been taken in part from police reports, and in part from my own speculations. It seems to me a strange turn of events when it's the junkie who becomes the historian and chronicles the doings of more legitimate citizens, but fact is often stranger than fiction. The following is no exception, for it involves Barry's shuffling off of this mortal coil, and the actions of the officers who helped him get there.

I'd actually met both of the officers responsible for ending Barry's escapade. They had been two of the cops on the scene when Cole killed Gerald. The first was none other than Logan County Sheriff Jim Bozeman, who had been dealing with Barry and his exploits for many a year now. The other officer was Deputy Glenn Jones, a longtime friend of Jim's. Both of them had been on the force for over twenty years, and like all cops in Logan County, the Flats were their cross to bear. Ninety percent of the calls they got and the arrests they made came from that two square mile cesspool of humanity.

Jim and Glenn had seen as much human sadness as any big city cop, not that it was something they were proud of. What they were proud of was their country boy smarts and the simple but effective ethic that comes with it. To my knowledge they never abused their power, and as they cruised the back roads of the Flats looking for Barry they talked with the ease that old friends share.

"Kind of nice just cruising these back roads. Especially with all the chaos going on down in OKC right now," remarked Jim.

"Yeah, it is," said Glenn. "Of course, now that you've said it, it's surely been jinxed."

"That's probably true," agreed Jim, then paused before adding, "I certainly hope someone else finds Barry first. He's a real piece of work, that one."

"You don't want all the glory for yourself?" Glenn jibed.

"There'll be no glory in it. I assure you," Jim solemnly replied.

"I was just funnin' ya a little," elaborated Glenn. Jim reached for the radio.

"I know," he said as he grabbed the mouth piece. "I'm gonna jump on the radio and see if Michelle has heard anything yet."

Just as Jim raised the mouth piece to his face they heard an explosion. Glenn hit the brakes, and they stared out the window at a rising plume of smoke less than a quarter mile away.

"That came from Hollister's place," observed Glenn. He was right about that. They were seeing the results of Barry's test with one of the sweaty sticks of dynamite.

"I bet that's our boy then," he said, then gave his partner an earnest look. "I really should have just kept my mouth shut."

Glenn hit the gas, and Jim spoke into the radio.

"Michelle, this is Jim. Over."

He only had to wait a second for her crackly reply.

"Copy. I'm right here. Over."

"We just saw on explosion coming from near the Hollister place so send some back up as soon as you can. Me and Glenn are gonna go check it out. Over."

"Copy that."

Glenn zipped around a corner and sped towards Hollister's.

"Slow down," said Jim. "I don't wanna kick up too much dust. Might let him know someone's coming. I'd much rather surprise him."

Glenn did as he was ordered, and they slowed to a crawl as they got near Hollister's property. His double wide and most of the junk was obscured by thickets of trees.

"Go ahead and block the end of the driveway," advised Jim. "It's a long curvy one if I remember right so he won't see the car."

Glenn eased up and put the car in park. They both turned and grabbed the two shotguns that hung on a rack behind their heads.

"Ok, quiet now. No slamming your car door," said Jim, as much to himself as to Glenn, who'd gotten used to Jim's habit of saying out loud just about anything that crossed his mind.

The two officers exited the vehicle, watching and listening for any signs of activity.

Bang! They heard a gunshot. It was the one Barry shot into Hollister's leg. Of course, they didn't know that so they ducked down in a hurry.

"Shit," said Glenn. "Was that at us?"

"I don't think so. Too far away and too many trees between us. I should get back on the horn."

Jim reached into the open car door and grabbed the radio.

"Michelle, Jim again. We've got shot's fired. Repeat, shot's fired. How far out is my back up? Over."

Bang! Another shot rung out. Jim didn't get an immediate reply from Michelle and got impatient in a hurry.

"Michelle? You there? What the hell's going on?"

Finally, he got an answer just as Barry's third shot echoed through the trees.

"Copy, Jim. You're nearest backup is about ten minutes out."

He and Glenn exchanged a look. That's not what either of them wanted to hear at the moment. There was another pair of officers searching the Flats, but they'd come across a belligerent drunk driver who had a gram of crank on him, along with his wife and three kids. Suffice it say they were currently preoccupied.

"You've got to be shitting me," remarked Jim. "Michelle, just tell them to get their asses here as soon as they can. Over."

"Copy. Over."

Jim tossed the mouth piece onto the seat. He grabbed his shotgun and looked at Glenn.

"You ready to go in?" he asked. Glenn tried to peer through the trees.

"Ready as I'll ever be I 'spose. What do you think that explosion was about?"

Jim shook his head. "I don't know, but when we come up on him, you damn well be ready to shoot."

Glenn nodded. "Can do."

"All right," said Jim. "Let's walk nice and easy up the driveway. We'll just make noise if we try to go through the brush. If he comes out shooting and we have to circle him just watch the crossfire."

Glenn dropped a nod and the two walked side by side as quietly as they could up the gravel drive.

While Jim and Glenn made their advance, Barry was hefting the box of explosives back into the Camaro. He eased it ever so gently onto the seat, fully aware of the volatile state the still perspiring TNT was in. What he had planned was anyone's guess. I've taken enough liberties with the facts as it is, and I can only imagine what mayhem he would have done if he'd been able to proceed much further. Perhaps he had no plan at all and was simply going to drive around, chucking sticks at whoever stood in his way. Only God knows, and I'm sure he's washed his hands of the whole ridiculous affair.

After Barry managed to get the dynamite loaded back up without blowing himself to shit, he eased the door closed. He then lit a cigarette and took a few puffs while Hollister's corpse still oozed fresh fluids. When the necessary nicotine massaged his brain, he walked around to the other side of the car and got in.

Before he started it up, he pulled Hollister's .357 out of his belt and set it in his lap.

Jim and Glenn had just gotten around the first bend in the driveway when they heard the Camaro's engine start.

Jim had been prepared for that possibility and already had a plan.

"You jump behind that tractor, and I'll get behind this tree," he said, pointing to the spots that would place him on the driver's side and Glenn on the passenger's side. "When he goes by, we jump out on my mark."

"I should take the driver's side, Jim. I don't want you in the direct line of fire if he gets a shot off," said Glenn.

Jim wasn't having any of that.

"Don't you worry about me. I'll stick this mule kicker right in his face, and if he makes a move I'll do what I got to. You just be ready to do the same on your end."

"Alright," said Glenn reluctantly. He trusted Jim, but he was sixty three, nearly twenty years Glenn's senior, and spent most of his time at the station.

Whether things would have turned out different if their positions had been reversed is yet another matter of speculation that I will not delve into.

Barry drove nice and easy down the bumpy drive with one hand on the box to keep it steady. He sped up a little too fast and hit a hole in the road big enough to jar the box in his hand. His breath stopped in his throat, and his foot hovered above the gas pedal a moment before he relaxed and resumed his course.

Just up ahead he would be coming around a bend that was buffeted by an old tractor and a few big trees.

Jim listened close as the car approached. He had the shotgun pointed straight down, and saw by the ruts in the road he'd probably have to take a strong step forward to get his rifle right in Barry's face. He figured that was the only chance to save the kid's life. Lord knew if he so much as farted then Jim would kill him without hesitation. He knew the kid was dangerous well before all this went down. Barry was only twenty two, but he'd done three short stints at the county jail, two for batteries and one for possession of a "controlled dangerous substance".

Jim tensed as the sound of the car's engine seemed to grow to a roar. He leaned hard up against the tree. Across the road, Glenn waited like a steel trap.

The front of the Camaro came into his view.

He took a step back and waited till Barry was right beside him. The window was rolled down. Jim took a step forward and jammed the shotgun in Barry's ear.

"STOP THE CAR! STOP THE CAR!"

Glenn sprang from his position and put his rifle into the open passenger window.

"HANDS UP! PUT YOUR HANDS UP!"

Barry hit the brakes. The lid slid off of the box. He looked around in a panic as he was yelled at from both sides, with twin shotguns practically rammed up his ass. He lowered his right hand to his lap, where the .357 sat.

"PUT YOUR GOD DAMN HANDS UP!" bellowed Jim.

Glenn noticed the open box of dynamite on the passenger seat. Barry's hand tightened on his gun. Jim's finger tightened on his trigger.

"Jim! Wait!" panicked Glenn, but it was too late. Barry hit the gas and raised his pistol.

Jim fired.

Barry's head exploded. Bits of brain and shotgun pellets peppered the windshield and the dashboard. The car veered sharp to the right, zooming off the road and into a tree. The box slammed into the dash, and the resulting explosion sent Barry and the car up like the fourth of July. I'm sure he wouldn't have had it any other way.

Glenn was killed instantly. Jim was blown back, and somehow miraculously saved. Even so, he caught a piece of shrapnel with his stomach and would spend the next few days in the hospital, lost in the deepest depression he'd known since his wife died ten years before. He was turned deaf as a post by the blast, and would have to retire as Sheriff.

It's worthy to note that both Cass and Aaron heard the blast go off, as did many other residents of the Flats. But Cass and Aaron were perhaps the only two who immediately knew it must have something to do with Barry.

I can't tell you what his life ultimately meant or was worth any more than my own. What I can say is that it all could have been avoided. It cannot be underestimated how people become a product of their environment. That isn't to say we aren't responsible for our own actions, because we most certainly are. However, when our youth decide drugs and crime are better options than any others in life, then any kind soul has to ask that one simple question.

Why?

Well, here's my two cents. First of all, it's certainly not because of any inherent flaw or sinful nature in us. Like Desmond's crutch, that's a bullshit copout. The simple truth behind why poor kids are more likely to choose a bad way is because it makes them feel more empowered than any other available possibility. Getting a minimum wage job does not accomplish the same. Joining the military and serving a government nobody believes in anymore doesn't accomplish it either. Going back to school is laughable considering the education they got in high school. All the pretty words about living in a land of opportunity are just that – words.

The choices are pathetic, and that goes a long way towards making people pathetic. We're all told we're free, but a lot of folks do not really feel free, and they have no clear enemy to rally in defense of. Some blame the government, some the Devil, but all people really ever do is just blame each other. There'll be no peace from within or from without till we put that practice to rest.

CHAPTER 12

And now my story is almost over. Twelve short chapters are all that my life was worth. I suppose I could have said more about my childhood or about my mother, but I'm afraid I'd just come off sounding like a whiner. Sure, our childhood shapes us in numerous ways, but so does getting over it. And I'm pretty much over it so I got nothing more to say about it.

After I left Vicki, I drove about fifteen miles to a town called Santa Rosa to stop for gas. The whole way there my head spun in mad circles while my heart felt like it'd been trampled, pissed on, and then trampled some more.

I parked at the pumps and sat there for a spell before I could gather my thoughts well enough to get out. I had to fight the desire to fall into that paralyzing introspection known only to addicts and the mentally ill. I stood up and looked at the sun, then pressed the heals of my hands into my eyes till I saw spots. That did the trick. I felt presentable enough to walk into the store and ignore the suspicious looks the attendant gave me. I dug into my pocket and pulled out a wad of cash. I quickly counted it, and saw that I had about forty bucks left. I gave twenty of it to the attendant.

"Gas," I said and walked back out the door. I lit a cigarette and walked to the pumps, where I grabbed the nozzle, selected the regular grade, and popped off my gas cap. I stuck the nozzle in and squeezed the trigger while taking deep shaky drags off my cig.

The attendant came out of the store and approached me with a look of pure condescension. I knew the type. He looked like a fucking boy scout, but he had a stupid, mean look about him that said he liked to stir shit when he fancied himself the cowboy.

"There's no smoking allowed at the pumps, sir," he reprimanded, as if I was the dumbest turnip to fall off the truck. Unfortunately for him, I was in no mood to be talked down to. I pretended to ignore him and took another long drag.

The attendant took a step towards me, his posture clearly aggressive. He was bigger than me, but he didn't know what he was messing with. My whole body tensed tighter than a lug nut on a tractor tire.

"Sir, put out the cigarette or I'll call the cops."

Before he even finished his sentence I yanked the nozzle out of my car and sprayed him with gasoline. Shocked, he back pedaled and fell right on his ass.

I hot boxed my cigarette and relished the look of horror on his face when I threw it at him. He cried out and slapped the butt in mid air, knocking it harmlessly to the ground. Only in the movies do lit cigarettes cause gasoline to ignite on contact. In real life the cigarette just goes out. I suppose for the gas soaked attendant that would be considered a good thing, but for me at the time it meant I wasn't through with him yet.

I moved in on him. He tried to get up, but I put my foot in his chest and pushed him flat on his back. I then brought my knee down on his diaphragm and knocked the wind out him. All the pain in me wanted to unleash itself on this man, who had done me no real wrong. I had to restrain myself from grabbing his head and bashing it into the concrete. Instead, I leaned over him like a vulture and yelled in his face.

"You just go ahead and call the cops, and I'll tell you what happens next. After I get out of jail I come find you, and I fucking kill you."

I lowered my voice and spoke again with pure menace. I noticed he wore a name tag.

"I even know your name, Rob. This is a pretty small town, and I don't think you're going anywhere are you? Even if you quit this job I could probably just ask anyone around here what happened to ole Rob who worked over at the Chevron, and *I bet your life* someone will be able to tell me exactly where you are, won't they, *Rob*?"

Now the guy looked scared. I wasn't done though.

"Would you care to know why I would do such a horrible thing?"

He didn't look like he did, but I told him anyway. It all came out in a mad rush.

"Because I'm a crazy piece of shit drug addict. But at least I know what I am. It's fucktards like you and the rest of the world that I feel sorry for. You're all just like me, and you don't even realize it. We're all a bunch of worthless addicts that need to get our shit together before we kill ourselves. Nobody's got any right to think they're better than anyone else. We're all fucking intangible… and I just put a gun to the face of someone who made feel a beauty I can hardly understand."

That last sentence came out of nowhere and trailed off. I sat stunned and absorbed what I'd just said. Out of that void came a deep resolve.

"I have to go find her," I said aloud, first to myself, and then I repeated it to the attendant, who stared into the eyes of a madman.

"I have to go find her, and you can't stop me. If you call the cops and stop me, you will be the enemy, and I will have to kill you. Be smart. Live."

I got off of him to let him up. He just lay there, afraid to move. I offered him some parting words of comfort.

"Look on the bright side. Now you have a crazy true story to tell your friends."

I turned and quickly went back to my car. I forgot to pump the rest of my gas, and I even left the gas cap lying on top of the pump. I drove away daring to hope that I might somehow find Vicki and make things right.

2

I turned onto the main street and went two blocks before noticing a small sign bearing the familiar profile of a greyhound dog. Thrilled with this discovery, I quickly cut over and turned where the arrow told me to go. I went two more blocks and saw the station. Across the street was a K-Mart parking lot, so I pulled in there and squeezed into a space with a clear view of the bus station's main entrance.

I told myself not to get too excited because there was just as good of a chance Vicki would get a ride past Santa Rosa altogether. I sat there wrestling with my fear and regret. I caught myself blindly fidgeting. I twisted the rearview mirror to look at myself.

I absently went to scratch the side of my face and saw a deep red mark where I had already been absently scratching away.

I stared at the mark in horror for a dozen eternities. Finally, I ripped my eyes away and reached for a cigarette. I lit up and looked around, suddenly paranoid that someone had been watching me. I tried to be inconspicuous. It wasn't particularly warm out, but I sweated like an all star. I began to tell myself that waiting here was stupid, that the chances of seeing Vicki were slim, and that the gas station attendant I accosted had probably called the cops anyway.

Ten more minutes of eternity went by. I again caught myself rubbing the same spot on my face. My mind went to dark places, and the veneer of my ego was stripped away. I sat there filleting my soul, telling myself I was worthless, that I was a fool, my life was hopeless, and that I was no outlaw, but an idiot. I began to cry, and I did not stop until I saw Ned's Lincoln pull up in front of the station.

When I saw Vicki get out of the car I was temporarily lobotomized.

I blankly watched her exchange brief words with the driver. Then she shed a wan smile and closed the door. She watched the car drive away and turn a corner before she did an about face and entered the station.

In a daze, I snubbed my smoke and got out of the car.

3

Vicki stepped inside and took a look around. Ned wasn't lying when he said it was small. It was only about five hundred square feet in its entirety; enough room for bathrooms, some vending machines, a few seats where a couple of other lonely travelers sat, and a counter where a bored clerk checked Vicki out.

She headed straight for the bathroom. She needed to splash cold water on her face and try to decide whether to get a ticket back to Oklahoma or to continue on to Cali.

Vicki pushed the door open and went straight to the sink. Another woman stood a couple sinks over and took note of Vicki's disheveled appearance.

"Are you okay, sweetie? I hope you don't mind my saying so, but you don't look so good."

Vicki looked over and gave her the same wan smile she'd left Ned with.

"I'll make it. Thanks," she replied. The woman wasn't convinced.

"Are you sure?"

The wan smile disappeared.

"No."

Vicki fought tears. The woman stepped closer and put a caring hand on her shoulder.

"If you need to cry, sweetie, go ahead and cry."

Her words were kind, but Vicki steeled herself, unwilling to let go.

"I'm tired of crying," she said. "I don't need to cry. I need to laugh. I need to laugh like a madwoman. I need to laugh like the gods are laughing at all of us."

The woman now offered Vicki her own wan smile and said, "Knock. Knock."

At first Vicki didn't understand what the woman had said, but then realization dawned. She hung her head and a deep hearty laugh escaped her.

"Who's there?" she asked.

"Doris."

"Doris who?"

"Doris locked, that's why I'm knocking."

Though she thought it was funny, Vicki didn't laugh again. She didn't have any left in her, but she was terribly grateful for the woman's kindness and humor.

"Thank you," she said. They shared a warm smile, and the woman touched her shoulder again.

"You're welcome, sweetie. I pray the good Lord sees you through."

Vicki nodded. She wasn't a bit religious, but she appreciated the sentiment none the less. The woman gave Vicki's shoulder a soft squeeze before she withdrew. She grabbed her purse and exited, leaving Vicki alone. She stood there for more than a minute, lost in thought before she snapped out of it and went about brushing her hair and washing the dried tears from her face.

4

I sat inside the station, waiting for Vicki to come out of the bathroom. I was in the front row of seats on the end, almost directly in front of the women's bathroom door. I half rose out of my seat in expectation when the kind woman came out first. Realizing it wasn't Vicki, I averted my eyes and plopped back down, disappointed. After that I had to wait another five minutes, which in my state was like waiting for California to drop into the sea. I was possessed by an anxiety so terrible I could feel my heartbeat in the back of my throat. I choked back rising bile and forced myself to sit as motionless as an exposed cockroach.

Finally, she came out and our eyes instantly met. I then experienced something akin to telepathic communication.

We were frozen in that moment. No words were spoken or needed to be. Our eyes told us everything we needed to hear. We conveyed how sorry we were and that we forgave each other. We said we wanted to keep going, together, and that it would all be okay. It was a miracle that I will never forget. To feel such hope is a both a blessing and a lesson.

I stood up and held one hand to her and one towards the door. She stepped to me and took the hand that was for her. We walked out of the bus station, oblivious to the curious stares of the other patrons.

That was the greatest moment of my life. From that day forward I would know that miracles can happen and that if there really was a God then he truly did love all of us equally. You may think I'm having delusions of grandeur, but if so, then perhaps you've never experienced salvation. It has a profound effect on a person, all the more so because it always happens in its truest form after we've reached some kind of low point. I know there are people who've had deeper lows than mine, but just ten minutes prior to this precious moment I felt like I was sucking mud up from the bottom. Now all that pain was a quickly fading memory. I was reunited with my crystal princess.

We exited and dashed across the street to my car. We hopped in, and I fired it up then threw it in reverse. When I turned to look behind me Vicki leaned over and kissed me. I hit the brake and returned her kiss. It was unlike any kiss I'd ever had. It was long, slow, and heavy with both passion and despair. My heart raced, but my mind slowed. It stirred my spirit but not my loins. I wanted it to last forever, but of course it did not.

We parted, and I pulled out of the K-Mart parking lot. I drove the two blocks back to the main street and turned towards the interstate. I got about halfway there when the cop zoomed into my rearview mirror.

Not good.

The gas station attendant had decided not to heed my warning. He'd been scared at first, but after a few minutes of deliberation he got pissed off and picked up the phone to rat me out. I suppose I deserved it, but at the moment I silently vowed to beat him down and shit in his mouth. Vicki saw the look on my face and turned to see who was behind us.

"Fuck," she whispered.

The cop's lights came on, and he burped his siren. I kept going, neither slowing down nor speeding up. Panic set in. In addition to the ensuing assault charges I had a used syringe on me, and Vicki was carrying some incriminating items as well.

The cop grew quickly impatient, and his siren blared full blast. I sped up.

"What are you doing?" Vicki barked in shock. She didn't know about my exchange with the attendant.

"When I stop you need to jump out," I told her. Her look said she couldn't fathom why I would say such a thing.

"What?"

I didn't have time to explain. I punched my car's tired v-6 up to 65. I was in a 35 zone so me and the cop zipped past the slower vehicles, which were fortunately sparse. The entrance ramp to the interstate was just up ahead.

"I'm going to stop, and you need to get out."

"You're kicking me out again?" she incredulously asked.

I only had time to say, "I'm sorry," before I had to hit the brakes to make the turn. I hung a hard left and skidded to a stop in the middle of the ramp.

"You have to go now. I'll be okay. I'll come back to the Flats when I get out of jail in a few months."

"Why are you doing this?" she demanded. This was all happening too fast.

"It's the only logical choice." I answered. The cop had stopped behind me, and he was already out of his car with his gun drawn, yelling at me to exit mine.

"You have to go now!" I yelled at her.

Finally, she accepted the out I was giving her. She grabbed her bag and for the second time that day she was dumped on the side of the road. As soon as she was clear of my car I threw it in drive and peeled away. The cop hesitated only a moment before running back to his car and giving chase.

I hit the interstate and pushed my car as fast as it would go, which according to the speedometer was about 105 miles per hour. I turned on the radio and cranked it as high as it would go to drown out the sound of the cop's siren. He was quickly right on my ass again, but I stubbornly drove on.

Then things went from bad to worse as my engine started to make a loud knocking sound. I turned down the radio to listen better. It sounded bad. I kept the pedal pegged, but the vehicle began to slow. I appealed to my car's finer sensibilities in the universal language of car owners.

"Come on you god damn whore!" I hollered, but it was no use. The vehicle slowed to 85, but I didn't let up. I was approaching a group of cars, and I committed an act of desperation. I didn't have room to pass on the left so I tore onto the shoulder and passed them on the right. Apparently the cop was equally determined in his efforts so he followed without hesitation. I skidded back onto the road between a little two door car and an 18 wheeler. The cop had to slow down to go behind the car, and I gained a little ground.

It wouldn't last two seconds.

The knocking sound in my motor made a devastating, fatal clang, and the engine cut out.

I screamed and slammed on the brakes. I was only four car lengths in front of the 18 wheeler when I screeched to a stop in front of it.

The semi hit its brakes, and the little two door car behind it slammed into it head on because the driver wasn't looking ahead. He was gawking at the cop that was trying to get around him. When his car hit the back of the semi, the truck jack knifed and flipped on its side as it hurled at me with a colossal scraping sound.

I braced myself for death, but the truck veered hard right, and instead of hitting me straight on, the back tire clipped my front end, spinning me around in a 180. I watched the decimated two door flip into the median as the cop car swerved to a crazy stop to avoid hitting it.

Then there was a moment of pure stillness. I think even my heart stopped beating. I could clearly see the cop through his windshield, and I imagined the bewildered, lucky-to-be-alive look on his face was similar to my own. But of course the moment passed, and the cop came to his senses. I watched him talk into his radio, and then jump out of his car. He drew his gun and walked towards me with such a look of fury that for a second I thought he might just shoot me. He began to yell at me to get out and lie down on the ground, but I ignored him. I found to my satisfaction that the radio still worked, so I cranked up the stereo and closed my eyes.

I'm not sure how long I sat there like that. I'm sure it wasn't nearly as long as it seemed. I thought about whether I should take my current predicament as a sign that I'd be smart to reconsider some of my life choices. I then realized my hand was rubbing the sore spot on my face again.

It was that more than anything that made me want to be done with crank then and there.

I jerked my betraying limb away and gripped the steering wheel with both hands. When you start literally pecking away at yourself, then some part of you is saying its time for a change. To help matters, my timing in reaching this decision appeared to be good, because my door was suddenly yanked open by someone willing to help me stop my bad habits.

The cop leveled the gun at my face.

"Onto the ground! Onto the ground!"

He was more amped up than I was. I wasn't trying to get shot so I took my hands off of the wheel and kept them where he could see them. I got halfway to the ground, and he rushed in on me. He brought the butt of his gun down on the back of my head.

That hurt.

The blow was quickly followed by one to the front of my head as I hit the ground.

That one hurt too.

He was on top of me in a flash to dig his knee into my back. He then twisted one of my arms behind me with the gentility of a howitzer. Next, my other arm was given the same treatment before I was cuffed and had my face ground into the road. The cop then felt obliged to divulge his general feelings on our sudden acquaintance.

"You're lucky there are witnesses, you fucking douche bag," he said in reference to the growing line of cars behind us. I gave silent thanks that I'd been spared a bad thrashing at the hands of this justifiably pissed off police officer.

I wondered how long I'd have to be in jail. I'd never done more than an occasional trip to the county jail for petty crime, the equivalent of summer camp to any real convict. That isn't to say I hadn't done things to warrant more time behind bars, as you now well know, but up to this point I'd had a pretty good track record as far as not getting busted.

Obviously, that was not the case this time, and I knew no judge would have mercy on me. What worried me the most was the driver of the small two door car. I feared he was dead. If so, that would mean I was on a whole other level of trouble.

When the cop's back up arrived I was hauled into the back of a state cruiser and left there for hours. My sick mind wandered, and I became lost in an endless parade of memories and dark fantasies. Sometimes I cackled like a lunatic, more often I cried, and occasionally I even dreamed of making love to Vicki as the flesh melted from our bones.

This was the fantasy I was currently engaged in when the driver's door opened and an officer sat down. The door closed, and he sat there writing on his clipboard for a couple minutes before putting it down. Then he turned and spoke to me through the metal mesh that separated us.

"You have the right to remain silent. If you - " he began, and I quickly interrupted him.

"What are you charging me with?" I asked. I had to know how bad it was.

He looked at me coldly and replied, "It's up to the D.A. to charge you. You are being arrested for..." he picked up the clipboard. " speeding, reckless endangerment – "

I again interrupted, "Just tell me if the guy in that car lived or not."

The officer put down the clipboard. His contemptible, pitying look of disgust told me the score before his words left his mouth.

"No. He did not."

Devastation reached out its gnarled, frigid hand and strangled my heart. I slumped onto my side like a discarded marionette, and my mind flickered through a numbing sequence of mini black outs. When that stopped I just laid there, mentally and emotionally annihilated. I remained in this vegetative state for the entirety of our drive.

I vaguely remember arriving at the police station and being booked. It wasn't until I was changing into orange jailhouse scrubs that my thought process finally resumed a steadier course, and then I could think of only one thing; that by the time I got out of jail, Vicki would be dead.

5

They gave me fifteen years.

I was found guilty on multiple charges. The most extreme was a conviction for manslaughter, which carried the bulk of my sentence. The next was aggravated assault on the gas station attendant. They also found the needle I had stashed in my shirt, and there was enough residue to get a drug charge. Then of course there was speeding, attempt to elude an officer, reckless endangerment, and a felony DUI.

When I was in court and the judge read the sentence, I stood stone faced, barely hearing his words. By that time I was beyond caring about anything, and I had accepted whatever fate the gods wished to hand down. I would do thirteen of those fifteen years and spend the duration of my sentence in the New Mexico State Penitentiary, one of the worst prisons in the country.

Vicki died about midway through my second year. I saw her twice in that time. The first time she looked more beautiful than ever to me, even though the mood and conversation were both somber. The second time, she looked like a walking skeleton, and my heart broke all over again. A couple months later I got a letter from her sister saying she had passed on. No details were given.

I fell into a deep depression. I would remain there until I was almost raped by two other inmates. I was assaulted by them inside that classic prison love nest – the shower. When they first grabbed me I just went limp, not caring what happened. Then some flood gate opened inside me, and I flipped the fuck out. I turned and grabbed one of the men by the head. I then quite literally bit his nose off. His screams and all the blood convinced the other one to abort the mission. I spent weeks in solitary. After I got out I was left alone for the most part. I still got my ass beat a few times over the years, but no one ever tried again to take my ass, if you catch my meaning. I spent most of my time reading and lifting weights. By the end of my fourth year I was no longer the skinny kid I used to be, and I considered myself well read.

But of course, don't go thinking I was on the road to rehabilitation.

No one can fathom the darkness that those serving long prison sentences are subjected to except those that have been there or are still there. No one. In my opinion it is a complete waste of time, but perhaps not for the reasons you might think.

It is a waste of time because it is a waste of justice. Prolonged incarceration lessens everyone involved; the criminals, the victims, their families, and even society at large. It is not a way to deal with crime. It is a way of not dealing with it. I caused someone to die, and it should be up to the family to decide my fate, not the state. I would have rather died myself or been subjected to cruel torture than be caged because of society's immature uncertainties on how to deal with people like me. Does anyone really think anything good comes out of prisons? What kind of people do you think emerges from these ovens after they've been baking for ten or more years like I did?

When I finally got released I was over thirty years old, and I'd never had a job in my life. I had no high school diploma and no GED because I had stubbornly refused any and all assistance from the state to formally educate myself while I did my time.

At no point did I ever have any intentions on rejoining society via the conventional routes. I am still an outlaw. It is an identity I will cling to till the day I die. If you are looking for a story about a man who turns his life around and finds Jesus then you just read the wrong book.

Once I was out of jail I was put in a halfway house. It took me less than a week to find a small time dealer who would front me some crank. The rest is history. I was hustling all over again, but to my credit this time I never took the drug, I never stole anything, and I bombarded the ears of my customers with my outlaw philosophy. I was soon making enough money to get a car and my own place. Ah, the American dream is alive and well.

I'd like to be able to offer you a more uplifting ending, but that's not how it usually works out in the real world for people like me. I'm also tempted to spend these last few pages ranting about how everyone else is to blame, but I hope by now you know me well enough to know that I think the blame game is bullshit. That virtue aside, I have not become a role model or anyone you'd probably want to meet unless you're in need of a fix, a whore, or a bag of good reefer. Because I live humbly I've never been busted again (knock on wood), and I am generally known as a kind person despite my career choices. Of course, taking my kindness for a weakness is not an advisable decision either, let's be clear about that, but situations where I need to assert myself are few and far between. I am fair to people and for the most part they are fair in return. That may surprise some folks, but as long there is honesty in any relationship it can prosper.

You may say that none of my pathetic ego fluffing matters and that I'm still a piece of shit, but I say I'm just playing the hand I was dealt. If that's a truth that some can't accept or wish to disregard as an absurdity then they'll hear no argument from me. I don't need to argue with fools. I likely know more about crime and its causes than you do; and I know damn well what the bottom line is when it comes to the principle cause of crime within the community. So in an effort to depart on a grand note, I'll leave you with that bit of wisdom.

The bottom line is that *there is no community*. If there was, then crime would be rare because people would be unified instead of divided. If we want to change the world, then *we* have to do it by talking face to face with each other. We must accept not just our neighbors, but our entire neighborhoods into our lives, and the only thing that will do that is communication. Funny how those two words, "community" and "communication" kinda look the same, huh?

The less time we take interacting with each other, the darker our lives will become. Even a fool like me can see that.

And now I think we are at the end. I can't tell you what the overall point of the story was or the underlying theme. If people who consider themselves more educated than me wish to evaluate it then they can go for it. I have no all encompassing moral to tell.

However, if I was backed into a corner with a flamethrower and told to sum it all up with one word, I suppose it would be this.

Grow.

CPSIA information can be obtained at www.ICGtesting.com
Printed in the USA
BVOW11s0236200814

363461BV00004B/15/P